May this book of prophetic meditations expand your measure of rule and cause for the favor of God to be greater on your life in this year.

In His Grip!

Apostle Michael Petro

RECONNECTING
WITH DIVINE GRACE

365 Daily Meditations to Transform Your Life

MTP
PUBLISHING

South Bend, Indiana

MTP
PUBLISHING

707 Sherman Avenue
South Bend, Indiana 46616
www.kingdomlifeccc.org

ISBN-13: 978-0692367216

TABLE OF CONTENTS

Dedication

I dedicate this book to my loving wife, Tina, and to my children, Brittany, Devin, Tobias and Jada who remind me every day how precious life is.

And to my mother Janice Hall: thank you for praying for me and keeping me before God,
And showing me how to love by your example, of how you love God.

I love you all very much.

~~~

Acknowledgements

I would like to acknowledge the following people for assisting me in the creation of this devotional.

To my wife, Tina, thank you for your love and support; and for being my inspiration and motivation to complete this book.

To my Kingdom Life Church family: thank you for allowing me to pastor you and in gaining the wisdom and understanding needed to write this book. I appreciate your loyalty to the vision of Kingdom Life.

To Sunamita Lim for her editorial vision and insights.

Thank you all for the love and concern you've shown.

FOREWARD

Since December 2002 when Apostle Michael and I started Kingdom Life Christian Cathedral, a great transformation has taken place in our lives as we have set out to be a family on a mission for God. We are thankful for the many opportunities that God has given us to impact the lives of men and women, not only in our local community, but in this region and abroad. There have been amazing high points and some incredible lows throughout our journey, but thank God for His comforting words, "I will never leave you, nor forsake you." No matter the situation we've faced, we've been victorious. And through the experiences that we've had, we've drawn closer to one another and have grown stronger in our faith in God. We have children that are just reaching teenage years and that brings on its own set of challenges. I am learning more and more how special they are and how much they sacrifice to ensure that the Word of God goes forth through us. Our adult daughter Brittany constantly reminds us that to love is of God and love always prevails. They are all very special and we never want to take them for granted. They're great "PC's" as our daughter, Jada has coined them– "Preachers Children"–which she believes carries a less negative connotation (from what she has heard) versus the not so average "PK" or "Preacher's Kids." I'm amazed at their maturity in how they understand their roles in the body of Christ. They're my heroes and great examples of unselfish sacrifice to achieve a Kingdom result.

This book was compiled from fruitful years spent in fellowship with the Lord. Many of these meditations and words of comfort and wisdom, in some form, have been shared with members of our church at much needed times of trial and turmoil in their lives. These words have provided relief and assured them that God loves them and has not forgotten them. He stands ready to provide help, hope and healing at the point of their greatest need. Over the years as Michael has been spending time in the presence of God, I am excited that he has been inspired to write what he feels necessary to draw the body of Christ back to Himself. As you read these meditations, you will sense a refreshing and a wooing from the Lord to get just a little closer to

Him. We're hopeful these mediations will speak life to your bones and be beneficial in reconnecting you to the divine grace of God. Allow this book to transform your life as you learn about the power of God and the wonderful plans He has for you to overcome every obstacle and gain victory in all areas of your life. I believe that as you read this devotional, day by day, you'll feel a deeper and more divine connection to the Almighty God. Spiritual goals have been established to guide readers through each month, beginning with "Getting Our House in Order for the New Year" in January. Scriptures within each devotional are meant to clarify the meditation and give it relevance for you, for that day. Italicized suggestions and questions guide you to reflect on, and apply them, to your personal situations. There is also a section to briefly note your flashes of inspiration. I encourage you to get a journal and keep it handy; when you run out of space, you can continue with the meditation or prayer and refer to the entries for inspiration and refreshing insights throughout the year. I thank Apostle Mike for his Pastoral oversight and leadership and for sharing this gift with the body of Christ. Please consider sharing this book with someone.

"And he who wins souls is wise." [Proverbs 11:30]
Pastor Tina M. Patton

INTRODUCTION

As founder and pastor of Kingdom Life Christian Cathedral in South Bend, Indiana, with my wife, Tina, I'm honored, humbled and grateful to share my spiritual journey with you with 365 days of unique meditations given to me by the grace of God. They're intended to encourage and uplift those who read them and are meant to bring you into a closer relationship with God.

They recount my own personal struggles that caused me to draw nearer to God and spend intimate time with Him for answers and encouragement. Through this process, I began to share them with others within the congregation and across the country. The response was so overwhelming that I sensed a need to share them even more widely—with this book.

Time spent with God is valuable and will add wisdom to your life. These bits of wisdom will provide hope and keep you motivated to press through whatever life brings you. For every issue or problem, there are solutions to be found in the Bible.

These meditations are beneficial in helping people gain a better understanding of what it means to live a Kingdom Life. A Kingdom Life is a life of blessings, hope and prosperity. My mission is to empower people to live better spiritually, mentally and physically. I want to inspire my church family, my natural family and anyone that I come into contact with to pursue every God-given opportunity afforded to each of us and to reach our highest potential in using God's spiritual gifts to the best of our abilities.

My goal is to motivate you to make unlimited progress with your own spiritual journey, by inviting Jesus Christ into your life; and as well, for your loved ones.

This book's format is part-journal. If you run out of space, continue with your heartfelt revelations in a separate journal. Stick with these daily meditations. Your efforts to continue connecting with God's Word is entirely up to you, at your own pace.

You'll also find that as your relationship with God deepens, He'll help you manifest your spiritual destiny with Jesus Christ as your eternal friend and Master. That's how I found my way with these 365 intimate meditations—at the Feet of My Master, Christ the Lord.

♥♥♥

JANUARY
DAY 1

As soldiers in the army of the Lord, we must walk with prophetic insight that will enrich us with spiritual wisdom. To be successful this New Year, we must learn what God's wisdom is for each of us. Solomon said, "Wisdom is the principle thing, therefore get wisdom." [Proverbs 4:7] We must have the same burning passion that Jesus had. Jesus said, "I must be about My Father's business." He was passionate about doing the Will of His Father. This year, we must expand the Kingdom in a greater way. How will that happen? By becoming more passionate about the work of the Lord. Jesus said, "I must work the works of Him who sent me, while it is still day." [St. John 9:4] Our time is now.

What are your goals for this New Year?
How will you awaken the wisdom within you to guide you in daily activities?
How will you apply practical wisdom to family, work and community?

My thoughts:

_____
_____
_____
_____

JANUARY
DAY 2

As we look to expand the Kingdom, we must also preach the Word. God said, "My Word will not return void." [Isaiah 55:1] Knowing that all of us have a responsibility to preach the good news of Jesus Christ, Paul exhorted, "Preach the word! Be ready in season and out of season." [II Timothy 4:2] It means to preach with equal urgency whether conditions are favorable or unfavorable—so that we see the manifestation of salvation, healing, signs and wonders. I encourage each of you to invite the Presence of God into every situation so that He may direct your paths according to His Will.

Soulfully offer a situation inviting God's Presence for His guidance and assistance.
Sincerely pray for Him to bless your actions with clarity and responsibility.
Then spend quiet time reflecting on His Presence to better hear His Word.

My thoughts:

_____

_____

_____

_____

JANUARY
DAY 3

The Lord's great grace is poised to rain upon the Church. As it was in the Book of Acts, so will it be for this year. This is the year when God will pull back the exterior of the Church to show His muscle. God will show his power through us against the enemy; so that we would take back what the devil stole from us. Get ready for a phenomenal move of God. [Acts 4:33]

What are you aspiring for this year, for God's Grace to shower upon you?
What will you do with this special blessing, to enhance your life? How will you share it?

My thoughts:

_____

_____

_____

_____

JANUARY
DAY 4

Prosperity will not come without a fight. The enemy will attempt to influence believers to operate in disorder, lawlessness and disorganization. We must be aware of these challenges, to be strategically aligned for the battles to come. As I release this prophetic word to you, I hope you'll place yourself to fight hard and not give up. Paul told Timothy, "Fight the good fight of faith."[1 Timothy 6:12] Be extra vigilant, as the enemy wants to snatch the faith of every Kingdom citizen.

Invoke God's Grace to bless you with solid faith—especially in the face of surmounting challenges.
What is the most pressing challenge you're facing now?
How will you approach and resolve it peacefully?

My thoughts:

_____
_____
_____
_____

JANUARY
DAY 5

Paul also said, "For the weapons of our warfare are not carnal but mighty in God." [2 Corinthians 10:1-5] Christians have been given weapons of the spirit, divinely designed to successfully wage war against Satan and unwholesome temptations.

What are your three most powerful qualities?
How have you used them to overcome challenges?
Reflect on how they have saved you, and give thanks.

My thoughts:

_____

_____

_____

_____

JANUARY
DAY 6

Spiritual expectations for believers in the Body of Christ are powerful lifestyle tools: 1) We must fight. 2) We must walk with prophetic and practical insight. 3) We must be passionate about carrying out His work. 4) We must preach the Word. 5) We must become more aware of His Presence in daily living. 6) We must walk in our God-given authority. As we continue with these expectations, it becomes an increasingly significant year for the Body of Christ—by remaining steadfast in Him.

How will you remind yourself to become more aware of our collective spiritual expectations?
To begin, how will you invite three expectations into your life, starting now?

My thoughts:

_____

_____

_____

_____

JANUARY
DAY 7

This is a day to declare with determination: "It's Going Down!" We've received our marching orders to fight the evil that's in us, as well as the evil around our homes. Paul said it best in Romans 7:19: "For the good that I will to do, I do not do; but the evil I will not to do, that I practice." Paul was being honest with himself and to the people of Rome to whom the epistle was addressed. [Romans 1:7] At some point, we must be honest with ourselves, too, in acknowledging our imperfections and limitations that we need to work on and bring under control.

What are three attributes that make you cringe when you see them in others?
Do you see any of these in yourself?
How will you deal with them, to gain better mastery and self-control?

My thoughts:

_____
_____
_____
_____

JANUARY
DAY 8

What a powerful witness Jabez is, to the Body of Christ, that anyone can move God, no matter what our situation. In Chronicles 4:10, we find Jabez calling on God to help him through his plight. He adamantly believed that God, and only God, could turn his situation around. The Bible says he prayed four powerful paradigms that were according to the Will of God:
1. Bless me indeed
2. Enlarge my territory
3. That Your hand would be upon me
4. Keep me from running to evil

1 John 5:14,15 informs us: "Now this is the confidence that we have in Him, that if we ask anything according to His Will, He hears us. And if we know that He hears us, whatever we ask, we know that we have the petitions that we have asked of Him." But, you first have to ask God before He can be moved. Scripture says: "Ask, and you shall receive." We also know Scripture says: "That you have not because you ask not." You **must** ask God for what you want.

What would you like to ask God for, today?
How will it help you and your loved ones, to turn around
situations such as health and finances?

My thoughts:

_____
_____
_____
_____

JANUARY
DAY 9

When asking God for anything, it must be out of a pure motive. We must continually ask ourselves this question to ensure we're not like the heathens who used vain repetitions to try and move God. So, in order for us to be able to garner tremendous results in prayer, we must meet these four conditions:

1. We must ask in Faith [Matthew 21:22]
2. We must be motivated properly [James 4:3]
3. We must abide in a relationship with Christ [John 15:7]
4. We must ask in accordance with the Will of God [1 John 5:14,15]

Then only can we do as Paul advised: "Be anxious for nothing, but in everything by prayer and supplication with thanksgiving, let your request be made known to God." [Philippians 4:6] And God will answer you. Cultivate petitions that move God!

What are your pure and sincere prayers at this moment?
It's helpful to take short prayer breaks throughout the day to reconnect with His Presence.

My thoughts:

_____

_____

_____

_____

JANUARY
DAY 10

As we enter this New Year, we should see the significance of the number 10 as it relates to our spiritual lives. In biblical terms, 10 represents: testimony, law, responsibility and the completeness of order. It signifies the completion of God's divine order. I know God wants to restore the lives of believers. For God to work through us, we must "Get Our House In Order." This means: pick up the clutter, throw out the trash, sweep and mop up and tidy up as best we can to more fully experience God's season of restoration. This year, we need to step up our prayer lives to become more persistent; and as well, more obedient. We all have struggles we need to address, to help us appreciate yet another dimension of God. When we step it up, we will be restored. To validate this prophetic Word of the Lord, read: 2 Kings 20:1-7. Look at the life of Hezekiah and how God dealt with him and turned his situation around. You, too, will be able to divinely overcome your challenges in God's own time!

Have you noticed the significance of the number 10?
If yes, in what ways?
If no, list 10 internal housekeeping items you'd like to clean up on.

My thoughts:

_____

_____

_____

_____

JANUARY
DAY 11

Prayer is in order as we kick off this new year. It's important that you increase your personal prayer time. Jesus said to the disciples, "Could you not watch with Me for one hour? Watch and pray, lest you enter into temptation. The spirit indeed is willing, but the flesh is weak." [Matthew 26:40-41] Prayer does not have to take up an hour straight, but can be broken up into multiple ways that add up. Precious time spent with God benefits you in nourishing your soul. This is a must, like water is for the human body. Without spending precious time with God, you'll die spiritually, with the enemies of your soul ultimately destroying you. Reading books on prayer such as this enhances your prayer life. Prayer is one of the most powerful and divine weapons God has blessed us with!

Keep a daily prayer journal.
Just short, simple notes will help you stay on course to nurture your spirit.
Read them regularly for inspiration and the motivation to continue.

My thoughts:

_____

_____

_____

_____

JANUARY
DAY 12

As the Lord releases great grace unto the Church, it's important for each of us to take on the mind of Christ wisely. The word "great" is the Greek word meaning mega and the word "grace" is "charis," which also means unmerited favor. We're beyond unmerited favor because in this case, Acts 4:33 deals with operating out of the power and authority given to us as Charismatic Christians. We're the sons and daughters of God who have been chosen to walk as Mega Charis believers. Simply put, if you've been filled with the Holy Spirit, you are a Charismatic Believer gifted to operate with the gifts bestowed upon you by God—regardless of your denominational affiliation. Each one of us, as Charismatic Christians, must walk in our calling so we're effective and efficient in expanding the Kingdom of God.

How will you share your gifts of grace with your family?
How will you share them at work?
How will you help expand the Kingdom of God in your community?

My thoughts:

_____

_____

_____

_____

JANUARY
DAY 13

When we talk about "Kingdom Momentum," we understand it to be a spiritual force that's released through obedience to the direction of the Holy Spirit. This sets in motion an ever-increasing divine participation to overcome adversity—to accomplish Kingdom objectives. From the beginning of time, God has set in motion His momentum in bringing forth undeniable results. But the prerequisite for believers to experience results is based upon obedience. Isaiah said: "If you be willing and obedient you can eat of the good of the land." [Isaiah 1:19] Obedience to God causes a spiritual momentum to take place in your life that becomes unstoppable. From the Old Testament to the New, you'll find a pattern that solidifies this truth. One of Job's friends (Elihu) told Job if he wanted to see results he had to be willing to obey and serve God. "If they obey and serve Him, they shall spend their days in prosperity, and their years in pleasures." [Job 36:11]

Divine obedience is not blind obedience. It means having faith in God by loving and serving Him.
Offer your life to serve divinely with your purest aspiration to see, feel and do good things only—for yourself and others.
What are your hopes for contributing selflessly towards building our Kingdom Momentum?

My thoughts:

_____
_____
_____
_____

JANUARY
DAY 14

God's momentum enables believers to make progress, and to advance in experiencing the goodness of the Lord. Joshua and the children of Israel experienced Kingdom Momentum in Joshua Chapter 6, when God told them to take the city of Jericho. He gave them instructions on how to do it, even though the enemy had other plans. For God resolved that they would take Jericho. They obeyed the plan, which created spiritual momentum; and on the seventh day, the walls of Jericho came tumbling down to give them the momentum needed to take the city.

Gaining spiritual momentum enriches our lives with God-blessed victories.
Reflect on what happened in your life when your obedience enabled you to overcome adversity.
Recalling these events can enrich and nourish our lives and spirit!

My thoughts:

_____

_____

_____

_____

JANUARY
DAY 15

There is a process of change, for personal and spiritually based transformation. These are recommended steps to become a leader in the Kingdom of God:

1. Make a decision
2. Turn your will over to God, totally
3. Be possessed with a strong desire to change
4. Deepen your knowledge base to understand what needs to be done
5. Look into the word as a mirror to change
6. Diligently apply the truths you learn, day by day
7. Guard the entrance to your heart with positive thoughts
8. Defend your mind against old thoughts
9. Be selective of what and who you expose yourself to
10. Dis-associate from the past
11. Be open to correction, new suggestions and be teachable
12. Depend on God and others for support

Anyone can do it. Just try!

My thoughts:

_____

_____

_____

_____

JANUARY
DAY 16

Process gives us as believers the chance and the ability to prove that what is good, acceptable and perfect according to the Will of God, can work for us. "Beloved, be committed, stay in the process and walk in the newness of life as you make your call and election sure; for if you do these things, you will never stumble." [2 Peter 1:10]

Committing to a spiritually based personal transformation is exciting! This process is life-changing to allow you to see and welcome new possibilities.
Note how walking in the newness of life impacts you and those around you.

My thoughts:

_____

_____

_____

_____

JANUARY
DAY 17

We're mega Christians with the ability to express the very attributes of God. As a man or woman of God, we're gifted spiritually—which makes us a charismatic people. With that in mind, God released great grace to the Church in Acts 4:33 that we would be a people of "megadunamis." The Greek word dunamis means power; given to us by God as we live our lives here on earth. Individually and collectively, we must be about our Father's business to combat darkness, to brightly shine our light, so that people may see the light. I encourage you today, to start walking in mega power to see the transforming power of God operating in each of us. This will produce an apostolic and prophetic move of God in our region, like never before!

Reflect on the mighty mega-dunamis powers you're gifted with. Be inspired to stretch them even more when facing new challenges!
What other qualities would you like to develop? Just be patient with yourself in being persistent, so you allow time for the seeds of your aspiration to sprout according to His Will.

My thoughts:

_____
_____
_____
_____

JANUARY
DAY 18

Paul recognized he was dealing with struggles that were three-fold. First, things from generations past (generational curses); second, his upbringing as a Pharisee; and third, his own personal sin issues. He said, "If I do what I will not to do, it is no longer I who do it, but sin that dwells in me." Everyone has issues to address and to work through, in every season of our lives. Whether it's lust, low self-esteem, fear, anxiety, drug addiction, sexual immorality, pornography, or a habit of lying, these issues wage war against our minds, thus causing us to be captive to the law of sin. Paul cried out: "O' Wretched man that I am! Who will deliver me from this Body of death?" You will, Lord! As we go about each day, we must learn to discipline ourselves to discipline our flesh on a daily basis.

Be not afraid to recognize your limitations.
Call them out and accept them for what they are now—so you
can move on to discipline them outwardly with courage, hope
and faith in the Lord's Own Way.
Bravely journal your weaknesses and record your successes in
working through them. Again, be patient with yourself and have
faith in Him to help you power on!

My thoughts:

_____

_____

_____

_____

JANUARY
DAY 19

There is power in prayer! Sometimes we forget how powerful the weapon of prayer is. The Bible says, "The weapons of our warfare are mighty in God." We must pray as Jesus did, to get the kind of results He did. Jesus prayed every morning before his day started for five hours. That's why the disciples asked Him to teach them to pray because they saw that when He prayed in that divinely intense manner, it resulted in a two-second healing throughout the day. That it would manifest deliverance in five seconds to someone within the day was awesome! Jesus always prayed before he ever got His day going, thus resulting in spending very little time on any problem that was presented to Him. Jesus is our pattern; do as He did and spend less time on a problem!

What wonderful and practical examples Jesus showed to the disciples that are still relevant for us today!
Prayer doesn't mean only getting down on your knees in church. Prayer can spontaneously happen whenever you feel moved to call upon the grace of God to help, heal and protect you and yours.
And always, end your prayer for help according to His Will Be Done.

My thoughts:

_____
_____
_____
_____

JANUARY
DAY 20

There are some natural things in our lives that God wants us to address, as we "Get Our House In Order for Him." In 2 Kings 20:1-7, the Prophet Isaiah said to Hezekiah that he needed to get his house in order. Now the text tells us that Hezekiah was a man who was prayerful, loyal and good. Through further reading, we find Hezekiah was the best King that Judah had ever had. Now Hezekiah was sick and unto death for no apparent reason. Therefore the Prophet spoke a word of doom over his life and to tell him, that the Lord needed him to get his house in order, first. When Isaiah spoke this word, he was telling Hezekiah that he needed to get his natural house in order and to line up his house in such a way that those who stepped in after his death would not have a difficult time handling his personal business. Now I believe God is speaking to each one of us about getting our natural house in order, too.

Let's be honest in cleaning up and setting in order our own house, literally and metaphorically.
What are two consuming concerns you need to address at this time?
If you've been putting off facing them, now is the time to meditate on God's grace to help you define and implement strategies to resolve them to His satisfaction.

My thoughts:

_____

_____

_____

_____

JANUARY
DAY 21

There are five things I would like for each of us to consider as we position ourselves in the Lord for the upcoming year. First, ensure our faith is in order by doing a spiritual check-up from top to bottom, to be sure we're wholly committed. Second, sit down and create a vision for you as family or single person to run with it, so it comes to pass! Third, to get family affairs in order, such as: health insurance, life insurance, taxes and business ventures—that you may prosper and be in sound health, even as your soul prospers in making divine progress. Fourth, getting our finances in order: bank accounts, investments, 401K, investment properties and savings accounts, so they flourish. Lastly, get your funeral celebration in order, so that there would be less stress for those who would have to step in to manage your affairs without going through a stressful probate process. I believe these are major areas that each of us should evaluate as we get our natural house in order.

Close your eyes and invite the Lord's Presence to help you develop a strategy to prioritize what needs doing.
Ask His Guidance for practical help to implement your strategy with the pros and cons you're facing.
Continue doing this diligently every day to better hear His Word.
Be sure to take notes because we forget easily.

My thoughts:

_____
_____
_____
_____

JANUARY
DAY 22

Paul addressed his young mentor Timothy when he most needed encouragement. Timothy had become a little timid in serving God because of the backlash he experienced with his calling. Paul reminded Timothy that it was a norm to suffer for Christ's Salvation. [2 Timothy 1:3-12] He quickly turned Timothy's attention to his present situation in Verse 8 that he was currently a prisoner because of his willingness to serve and preach the Gospel. So Paul, led by the Holy Spirit, gave young Timothy instructions on how to overcome fear in his life. Paul reminded him that God never gave him the timidity that he was feeling. It either came from his own emotional baggage or from the pit of hell itself. Instead God equipped him with love, power and a sound mind—the tools for daily living. Because God has equipped us, He instructs us to "not be ashamed ... but share in the sufferings." [2 Timothy 1:8] God gave Timothy (and us!) everything we need to accomplish the job. He empowers us before He ever expects anything from us. He gives, before He demands. We receive His competence, even before we receive His commands.

Such is the power of God's love in equipping us with great tools to face life's ups and downs!
What are some powerful emotional tools you've used to make progress at home and at work?
Offer gratitude so you become even more aware, and in the process strengthen their efficacies.

My thoughts:

_____
_____
_____
_____

JANUARY
DAY 23

God's desire has to become our desire, too. Paul said, "We must desire the best gifts." [Corinthians 12:31] This suggests we take conscious action to know ourselves spiritually. Each one of us is divinely gifted and have a place that we operate out of—that makes us most effective in working for His Mission. As believers, we must work on these gifts so we continue maturing and rising above mediocrity. We must always be engaged and not idle in wasting away His gifts—especially and whenever we come up against adversaries desiring to sift us off course as wheat in changing winds.

What are your best gifts that you honor family with?
What are your best gifts that you honor your workplace with?
How do you put your best gifts towards good purpose in your neighborhood?

My thoughts:

_____

_____

_____

_____

JANUARY
DAY 24

Remember, "Good is the enemy to great." Invite and allow the Lord into your life by recognizing that it's not enough just to be, "good." God wants to take you to a greater place, to experience Him more profoundly, where you can experience His joy like never before. Let us recommit ourselves to the things of God, to return to our first love as Revelation 2:4 tells us—in striving for greatness while doing His Work.

Spend a few quiet moments each day reflecting on God's greatness.
Ask for His Guidance to fill you up with whatever He desires at that moment.
Then give thanks and allow time for Him to work His miracles in and through you.
Note how your soulful invocation keeps making good things appear in your life.

My thoughts:

_____
_____
_____
_____

JANUARY
DAY 25

We must make sin become a slave unto us, instead of us being a slave unto it. Because if we don't, it'll disqualify us from the prize that God has laid up for us. Paul said, "No, I beat my body and make it my slave so that after I have preached to others, I myself will not be disqualified for the prize." [1 Corinthians 9:27] Each one of us has the ability to bring forth some discipline to our flesh. This is important because God doesn't want us soiled. He wants us to be as a tree planted, purified, strengthened and nourished by the waters. That's why we can say this year, "It's Going Down" because we're proactive in fighting the enemy. Now, be like Paul and say today, "I have fought a good fight!"

What would you like your life's mission to be, according to divine gospel?
Reflect soulfully on what you'd like to strive to achieve with the next 340 days of this year.

My thoughts:

_____
_____
_____
_____

JANUARY
DAY 26

There are so many barriers and distractions that have created hurdles in our prayer lives that keep us from experiencing and manifesting the Glory of God. As we enter this season of prayerful guidance from Him, we want to ensure that there are no hurdles there that would keep us from receiving the petitions we've laid out before God. Each of us have a responsibility to do our part during this season in not letting each other down. Jesus said to the disciples: "Could you not stay awake and watch with me while I pray one hour?"[Matthew 26:40] I pray that none of us have gone to sleep or gotten lazy during our time of petitioning God!

Stay awake and be focused on the moment of awareness each time you invoke and petition Him.
It helps to have paper and pen ready to record flashes of insights and epiphanies as they flash upon your consciousness.

My thoughts:

_____

_____

_____

_____

JANUARY
DAY 27

As we seek God for a word to sustain us this year, what Paul spoke to Titus in the Book of Titus is appropriate to hang our hats on. Paul said in Titus 1:9: "Hold fast the faithful word as he has been taught, that he may be able, by sound doctrine, both to exhort and convict those who contradict." Paul is simply saying that if we're going to be able to instruct believers and confront false teaching, we must remain sound in the faith. We must be cognizant of the fact that the enemies of our souls want to pervert us as believers to thwart God's Momentum. The enemy knows that if he can get us to compromise our faith, he can zap the strength of our testimony. The enemy doesn't mind us having a form of godliness because he knows we'll deny the miraculous power of God. So we must fight for the good of our faith by being a good example to believers, and as well, for those who are not.

How will you greet, and show kindness, to strangers?
When did you benefit from compassion extended by others?
Offer gratitude to the Lord for His munificent gifts benefitting all humankind.

My thoughts:

_____

_____

_____

_____

JANUARY
DAY 28

You must consistently assemble yourself in the House of the Lord. Being disconnected from the House that God called you to, will cause you to begin to compromise your faith. Things that you didn't do when you were faithful, you may find yourself indulging in now that you have no leader, no word and no prayer life to keep you sound in His faith. God uses the God man to set things in order in your life. But when you're not rooted in an assembly or church, it's impossible to do it. If you'll adjust yourself and reposition back into the fellowship of saints, God will reveal His plan to you for tremendous, supernatural results in your personal life, family life, social life, professional life and financial issues. God wants you to be sound in the faith that you would experience His fulfillment in your life. Stay Sound!

Never ever be embarrassed to ask for His help to set up your divine home.
Ask Him to show love, forgiveness and peace of mind in setting your house straight—so you can discover what a joy it is to consistently live in wholesome grace.

My thoughts:

_____

_____

_____

_____

JANUARY
DAY 29

It's important to stay mindful for this year to produce an abundance of spiritual fruit. Every element that God has given us through the Fruit of the Spirit shall be pruned and cherished for increase this year. Hence, to see such manifestation, we the people of God must allow God's Word to show us areas in our lives that need order and organization to properly grow in abundance. Once we submit to the change we ask for, we must abide in Him, and His Word must abide in us. This gives us the ability and confidence to ask Him for anything, and the receptivity to receive according to His Will. The Bible says, "It shall be done for you." [John 15:7] Show yourselves to be followers of Christ this New Year. Be Fruitful Bearers of, and in, the Lord!

What are three specific goals you'd like to pursue and cherish this year?
With your sincere and intense prayers, ask to be shown how to implement them wisely.

My thoughts:

_____
_____
_____
_____

JANUARY
DAY 30

Paul told Timothy: "Preach the word! to be ready in season and out of season." What he was conveying was the need to stay sound according to when it was convenient or inconvenient to administer the word. There are times when people want to hear the word and times when people don't want to be bothered. Paul said: "For the time will come when they will not endure sound doctrine, but according to their own desires, because they have itching ears, they will heap up for themselves teachers; and they will turn their ears away from the truth, and be turned aside to fables." [2 Timothy 4:3,4] As believers, we must be ever so mindful that there are people who are messed up because they've been duped and have fallen prey to someone else's pipe dreams. So be watchful, yet willing to endure afflictions as they come, in doing the work of an evangelist in fulfilling our ministry. Somebody needs your soundness in the faith today. Be an evangelist and win them over to the Lord!

Have you considered what an honor it is to share God's Word with others?
When people turn you down, don't ever give up.
Wholeheartedly sticking with your resolve pays dividends.

My thoughts:

_____
_____
_____
_____

JANUARY
DAY 31

The word in Acts 5:12-16 talks about the power of the church. We establish the fact that the church is: You. "We are the temple of the living God." [2 Corinthians 6:16] As with any house, we recognize it has to be filled with furniture. Therefore, God fills and furnishes us with His Holy Spirit and the Word. Once we have gone through God's process of becoming Kingdom Citizens, we begin to walk as one empowered and unified church. As the empowered church, we now have the ability to cast out demons and lay hands on the sick that they will recover, according to His Will.

Accepting God's Will Be Done is the loftiest goal to strive for and to achieve.
Invite God to furnish and decorate your home with sound, loving activities bringing family and friends more closely to each other. Celebrate His Grace with joyful Gratitude at every moment!

My thoughts:

_____

_____

_____

_____

FEBRUARY
DAY 1

Power brings forth dramatic transformation in the lives of people. Increasing power draws more people to church, which then causes and allows the church to grow naturally. Luke said in the Book of Acts: "That after the Holy Spirit has come upon you, you shall be witnesses to me in Jerusalem, and all of Judea, and Samaria, and to the end of the earth. For our first priority is to work in Jerusalem." [Acts 1:8] As we impact those within our reach with the power that we walk in, we will see great works and transformational exploits along with miracles, signs and wonders.

When was the first time you experienced a miracle?
What made you become aware of it and its impact on your life?
Has anyone thanked you for being a miracle-worker or angel in showing them light?

My thoughts:

_____

_____

_____

_____

FEBRUARY
DAY 2

God always gives us what we need to lead wisely. Paul reminded Timothy that God didn't give him the timidity he felt; that it came either from Timothy's own emotional baggage or from the pit of hell itself. God equipped him with love, power and a sound mind. All leaders need three fundamental tools to lead. **Love:** The relational ingredient that enables us to attract and connect with others. **Power:** The courage and competence to get the job done. **Sound Mind:** The perspective and wisdom to grasp a vision and take the right steps to benefit everyone. Because God has so equipped us, He instructs us to "not be ashamed but share in the sufferings." [2 Timothy 1:8] God gave Timothy (and us!) everything we need to get the job done. He empowers us before He ever expects from us. He gives before He demands. We receive His competence before we receive His commands. [2 Tim 1:7,8] Serve and Lead!

This meditation is similar to January 22. Why repeat it? Because it's important to understand and value why God has selected us and bestowed upon us these choice gifts to serve and lead.
As a leader in family and community affairs, reflect on how you lead with love, gentle power and a sound mind.

My thoughts:

_____
_____
_____
_____

FEBRUARY
DAY 3

Every day is a day of engagement for the people of God. We should wake up ready and eager to take on the wiles of the devil and hostile forces seeking those they can devour. As believers, it's essential we put on the whole armor of God to be battle-ready daily. Then we must march into our new day with a focus on God and what He desires for us to do. We also must not fear the unknown, for God has not given us the spirit of fear. Instead, dwell on God's gifts of: love, power and a sound mind. Once our faith has risen, then we must believe that no weapon that is formed against us will prosper.

Never ever fear the unknown. Instead, welcome God's Presence to guide you through the day.
Offer your heartfelt gratitude to be a dedicated instrument capable of donning on God's armor.
Whenever fear strikes, get rid of it by simply offering it to God, so He can transform your consciousness into awesome courage to tackle any crazy issue that inadvertently arises.

My thoughts:

_____

_____

_____

_____

FEBRUARY
DAY 4

As we go about our day, remember that we're are a powerful church that has the ability to walk in the dimension of boldness that God has released onto us. Boldness gives us the ability to walk in supernatural authority, which in turn gives us the ability to confront the unfortunate hostile attacks of this world. As you confront demonic influences with prayer and divine confidence in God's protection, your deliverance ministry acquires great power. And great grace shall be released unto you, to further release any misguided thoughts that may be holding you captive.

Always look for the positive in every situation.
Become a turn-around superstar whenever worries, anxieties and bad news surface.
Look for the silver lining in unfortunate incidents as lessons for strengthening your resolve to forever live positively in His Grace!

My thoughts:

_____

_____

_____

_____

FEBRUARY
DAY 5

"Sight is a function of the eyes, while vision is a function of the heart" is a quote from Myles Munroe's book, *The Principal and Power of Vision*. Sight is the ability to see things as they are, while vision is the ability to see things as they could, or should, be. We must never let what our eyes see determine what our hearts believe in. Faith is vision in the heart. Sight without vision is dangerous because it has no hope. The visions in our hearts are greater than the environments around us. God gave us vision so we would not have to live by what we see. We were created to live according to the way God wants us to function. God functions through faith and His Word. While thoughts are important, words are the most powerful for inspiring good action and service. Thoughts design a future, but words create that future. Whether words are spoken or written, they're full of creative power. Ideas control the world. A vision is an idea that is so powerful it can live beyond the grave. Learn to develop your faith from your heart!

What is your heartfelt vision for your life's mission?
How will you materialize or operationalize your life's mission?
Pray for wisdom and guidance to guide your practical
manifestations and activities.

My thoughts:

_____
_____
_____
_____

FEBRUARY
DAY 6

We must have a mindset for prayer at all times. We must continue to maintain that discipline if we're going to experience perpetual increase by the Holy Spirit this year. Each of us must do our part in the area of prayer so we cover our neighborhoods and regions to walk in our God-given authority. We must step up our desire to want to pray as the pattern was set in the Old and New Testaments. When Solomon dedicated the Temple unto the Lord, he did it through prayer. "If My people who are called by My name would humble themselves and pray and seek My face and turn from their wicked ways, then I will hear from heaven, and will forgive their land." This important prayer will get you Kingdom results beyond your wildest imagination. [2 Chronicles 7:14]

List the ways you can slip in moments of prayer during the day. Such as an intense minute of prayer for protection behind the wheel before driving off; then another minute of gratitude upon safe arrival at your destination.
Multiply the number of trips each day, and see how fast and easy it is to pray, by slipping in practical ways that do increase your prayer power!

My thoughts:

_____

_____

_____

_____

FEBRUARY
DAY 7

This is the day to give great witness to the resurrection of our Lord and savior, Jesus Christ. As we walk in the great power that the Lord has released to us, each of us can proclaim to someone else about His goodness and His saving power. God has given us great grace to walk divinely, so that we would have an effective day in Him. Ask God to allow you to cross the paths of those who need to be helped and ministered to, through your spiritual ministry. Thank God that we will not be intimidated—but that we will walk in His power, love and a sound mind.

Take time to pause, especially when running errands.
Be focused on running errands safely; but also please look out for those in need of your emotional and spiritual support.
How many persons were you able to reach out to today, with pure intentions?

My thoughts:

_____

_____

_____

_____

FEBRUARY
DAY 8

We have always had this precious light shining in our hearts. But we're like fragile clay jars containing this great treasure. It's very clear that our great power is from God, not from ourselves. And while pressed on every side by troubles, we're not easily crushed. We may be perplexed, but cannot be driven to despair. We may be hunted down, but never abandoned by God. We may get knocked down, but not destroyed. [2 Corinthians 4:7-9] Every soul and body is a unique vessel God has lovingly created for sharing with others. This treasure, referred to as the Gospel of Jesus, is contained in "fragile clay jars." Paul uses the phrase "fragile clay jars" because as humans we can be easily broken as we struggle with the most basic details of life. Yet, we're called upon to pour out our heart's treasure so the world connects with God.

It's important to get away from what the mind or ego desires, and to welcome God's Light deep within us that's waiting to be ignited, to light up our hearts.
Once we've connected with our own treasures from within, it's a divine responsibility to share them with other people.
And that's how we continue building the Kingdom of God as Kingdom citizens.

My thoughts:

_____
_____
_____
_____

FEBRUARY
DAY 9

God's good works flow naturally from a person whose life is totally committed to Him. [Matthew 15:18] The key is to give liberally of what we've received, knowing that the Lord will continue to fill us with even more blessings, so we're never totally empty nor constantly overflowing. Instead, our container will be full of holes that will continuously pour out the love of Jesus Christ. As long as we're being filled by God daily, we'll never have a problem serving those he wants us to serve. [Galatians 6:10] However, these clay jars can eventually become empty from lack of use. Empty vessels serve little purpose other than taking up space. And the Lord doesn't want us to simply exist as hollow vessels. Each person has been made for a unique purpose. When a follower of Christ is not connected to the source of these gifts, his or her desire for serving God and other people diminishes. Think about your life-vessel today. How has it been used to store the goodness of God? Has that goodness flowed into other lives? Has God's measure of goodness in you evaporated from days and months of non-use? Or is your life a container full of holes, leaking the goodness of God continuously because you're continuously filled by the Source that never runs dry?

Every day, ask for the Lord's guidance to carry out His Will. Simple, heartfelt prayers are all that's needed to refill our heart vessels.

My thoughts:

_____

_____

_____

_____

FEBRUARY
DAY 10

Do we see us as spiritual "low lives" in Christendom? Jesus was the perfect example when He chose to wash the feet of His disciples. [John 13:3-11] Jesus hosted a gathering before His death where he fed the disciples, as well as shared in Communion with them. In those days, when you gathered for such an occasion, the host was responsible for providing a foot wash for guests. This responsibility was always the task of slaves considered to be "low lives" of the community. They were treated as despicable people who were worthless, with a low social status. But Jesus recognized there were no slaves at the time, so He took it upon Himself to become a slave—to do what others thought was beneath them. Jesus said, "I came to serve, not to be served." So He became a servant unto them that they could see an example of a Servant Leader. One who will set down His title, position and influence to get the job done, no matter what others thought. Will you do likewise for the sake of ministry? If you answered yes, you're a shining inspiration as a Servant Leader!

Don't allow people to "low life" your selfless service in baseless, useless ways.
Instead, take the spiritual high road and be a determined, dedicated Servant Leader who inspires others to take the higher road to serve many others, as well.

My thoughts:

_____

_____

_____

_____

FEBRUARY
DAY 11

The Bible proclaims in Proverbs 23:7: "For as a man thinks in his heart, so is he." Believers must begin to think big, so we begin to see ourselves outside of the small places we've been holed up in. Some of us are indeed captivates of, and bound by, our small places of anger, loneliness, divorce, broken heart, family problems, shame and rejection. Even more scary is the question we've all asked: "Where is God in all of my problems?" Job was in a similar situation. But, you have to know that what's to come is better than all that has been. [Job 8:7] Because we are a people of faith, we must believe that nothing is too hard for God. [Jeremiah 32:17] We must: say it, decree it, declare it, expect it—and then act it. Afterwards, we must have information to properly deliver our promises to God. [Proverbs 11:9] Always keep in mind, The Greater One lives in you. [1 John 4:4] David said: "May the Lord give you increase more and more." What he meant was: May the Lord make you Bigger and Bigger in His image—but you have to begin the process—by Thinking BIG!

Start thinking BIG by setting more challenging goals to achieve for this year.
At the same time, self-evaluate your resources to be realistic in achieving your goals.
What are three BIG goals you'd like to aspire to?

My thoughts:

_____

_____

_____

_____

FEBRUARY
DAY 12

What is the work of the Lord? First, being in Church is good to begin the work of the Lord. Hebrews 10:25 says, "Not forsaking the assembling of ourselves together, as is the manner of some, but exhorting one another, and so much the more as you see the day approaching." Second, we must be soul winners as we live out our lives in the Lord's image. Matthew gives us an apostolic command to: "Go therefore and make disciples of all nations" including those who live with us, those in the workplace, in our neighborhoods and the market place, so they would be saved, too. [Matthew 28:19, 20] Third, we should be involved in Team Ministry. From Genesis to Revelation, God used the team concept for His Kingdom's business. From the very beginning we see the team concept in Adam and Eve. In the New Testament, we see the example of Jesus and His disciples; and as well, Paul and Silas. Plus many more. God never designed His business to be done alone. Perhaps that's why Ecclesiates 4:9 tells us: "Two are better than one." Fourth, we must be a people who are involved with in-reach and outreach ministry opportunities. As we get engaged with the business of the Lord, He wants us to be passionate about laboring for Him by working on our personal issues and issues with others. Remember, Jesus made the statement: "I must work the works of Him while it is still day, for night cometh when no man can work." [John 9:4] We must have that same urgency and passion to do the Will of God in our region and abroad.

How would you like to reach out to your neighborhood?
Would you like to practice practical ministry overseas? If yes, start praying for guidance.

My thoughts:

_____

_____

_____

_____

FEBRUARY
DAY 13

Jesus said in Matthew 21:13: "My house shall be called a house of prayer." This is significant because the only way to become a house of prayer is when we, the people of God, petition Him according to His Will. The Bible says: "If just two or three of you will come together, there will I be." [Matthew 18:20] The devil knows that if you ever catch on fire for prayer, he's in trouble. That's why things always come up when it's time for you to meet at church for prayer (or with others outside church) because he knows we'll be rendered powerless. I challenge you today to step up your prayer life, and to connect with other saints of God who will regularly spend time in prayer with you where you'll be in tune with prayerful practice. Fervent prayers of the spiritually righteous avail much!

Prayer is one wing of our soul bird when we petition God sincerely.
Meditation is the other wing—for quiet time to still the mind, to hear and feel God's answers.
Both prayer and meditation are needed to live richly and righteously in God's house.

My thoughts:

_____
_____
_____
_____

FEBRUARY
DAY 14

When you pray according to the will of God, 1 John 5:14,15 tells us: "This is the confidence that we have in Him, that if we ask anything according to His Will, He hears us. And if we know that He hears us, whatever we ask we know that we have the petitions that we have asked of Him." So just simply and humbly ask God as scripture advises, and you shall receive. But, you've got to ask!

When we petition God to light up our lives with His Will, we're not beggars.
Rather, we become more aware and engaged as His children in connecting with His infinite and never-ending gifts of: love, mercy, delight, hope, devotion and all manner of goodness.

My thoughts:

_____

_____

_____

_____

FEBRUARY
DAY 15

Consider the power of the blood Christ shed for us. Peter asked in Matthew 18:21: "Lord, How often shall my brother sin against me, and I forgive him?" Still today the question of forgiveness comes up in the mind of believers if it's something we haven't practiced in our walk with the Lord. The reply from Jesus was, "Not up to seven times, but up to seventy times seven, be forgiving." [Matthew 18:22] This is to say we should forgive others and ourselves unlimited amounts of times. It's the shed blood of Jesus Christ that separates us from our sins and redeems us from all unrighteousness. "He is faithful and just to forgive us of our sins, and to cleanse us from all unrighteousness." [1 John 1:9] Therein lies the power of God's love—in His blood.

God constantly forgives us.
Why is it so hard for us to forgive ourselves and other people?
It's important and healthy to learn to forgive from the heart.

My thoughts:

_____

_____

_____

_____

FEBRUARY
DAY 16

The primary and essential key to personal and professional success is—our prayer life. "The effective, fervent prayers of the righteous avails much." [James 5:16] If we're going to experience the tremendous blessings of the Lord this year, we must P. U. S. H. (Pray Until Something Happens!) Increase your time to pray and periodically fast so you may see the glorious manifestations of the Lord. God wants you to prosper and help you be even larger on earth so you can take authority over Satan and his temptations. God has already given us the victory. But we must now walk like the victorious people that we are. This is how we win God's victory for Him!

Allow yourself permission to spend time praying sincerely. No prayer ever goes unanswered. We just have to allow God's time to work in and through us. So also, learn patience—even as you step up your prayerful efforts.

My thoughts:

_____

_____

_____

_____

FEBRUARY
DAY 17

As Christians, we must live on the very prayers that we petition God for. Jabez in 1 Chronicles 4:10 is an example to us in, "Living On A Prayer." He called on the God of Israel to help him through a troubling time in his life. And God responded in a favorable way. The key to his success was that he asked God for what he needed—according to God's Will. Jesus said, "Whatever things you ask in prayer, believing, you will receive." [Mark 11:24] So if we're going to see God move on our behalf, we *must* ask. Whether small or large, engage God in all of your affairs and use His Word to speak what you need, for your petitions to bear fruitful existence and meaningful experiences.

Our lives are truly made of prayers.
Our ongoing petitions to live joyful and abundant lives are
spiritual efforts that will bear fruit in His likeness. God never
wants us to live a life of austerity or hardship.
So, stay the course with faith, courage, hope and gratitude.

My thoughts:

_____

_____

_____

_____

FEBRUARY
DAY 18

We must recognize that prayer is the greatest weapon in the believer's arsenal. It's through the discipline of prayer that we gain access to the power of Heaven's throne. We're always in the season of giving; not just giving the minimum requirement as Cain did, but giving God our very best, always. We overrule Cain's spirit and walk in the spirit of Abel who brought the appropriate offerings and the very best of his harvest. As we give of ourselves, substance and quality service, let's be mindful to give our very best because God gave us His very best—Jesus Christ—and used Him as "First Fruit" sacrificial offering to harvest you and I.

Honor your God-blessed gifts every moment, in everything you do.
Always strive to offer the highest and the finest.
While striving to offer the best, you'll find it's actually God striving in and through you to realize His highest.
What better privilege can there be, than to always invoke the highest, as His choice instrument?

My thoughts:

_____

_____

_____

_____

FEBRUARY
DAY 19

Prepare for Your Harvest. Make a greater effort to put God first in all things. As we do this, we can expect a fruitful harvest to come. Let us prepare our heads, hearts and hands, for the unlimited supply that God will release to every believer who gives unconditionally and affectionately to Him. Sacrificial obedience always provokes divine action which then activates the spiritual realm. As we prepare to bring God precious gifts like the little lad did with his lunch in John 6:9, God will show up and multiply it to release an increase back into our lives. We can then put a demand on our seed that will produce a harvest that entitles us to receive the grace of God.

This is a time to be prompt and excited about what God is doing; and as well, a time to seek Him that He would add all things unto you.
Give unconditionally and affectionately in obedience to God, and you will receive a great harvest.

My thoughts:

_____

_____

_____

_____

FEBRUARY
DAY 20

Fervent prayers put us on the offensive and set the tone for our seeing the manifestation of the Lord in great measure. The enemy attempts to render the Christian powerless, but by praying the Word of God over your situation, you can have powerful results of deliverance and healing in your life and for others around you. Don't underestimate the power of prayer in your life. Let us continue to walk in confidence knowing that as we pray according to His will that He hears us. And because He hears us, we shall have the petitions that we have requested of Him. [1 John 5:14-15]

Try to see beauty not as glitzy baubles of bling that we exchange for gifts.
Instead, appreciate the beauty of Christ's love and His manifestation in and through us.

My thoughts:

_____

_____

_____

_____

FEBRUARY
DAY 21

The Word of God is the seed we plant to harvest His blessings in the Kingdom of God. The sower sows the Word seed, so that the Word seed controls everything in his life. When God said, "Let there be light," [Genesis 1:3] the environment changed because of His Word. The Word establishes, forms and changes the natural world around us. Everything in our lives must either line up or get out when we stand on the Word. That's how powerful The Word is. Even when it looks as though it's not working, we have to stand tall on God's Word. When we've done all we can do to stand tall and strong, the Bible says we just have to keep on standing. We have to keep confessing, keep declaring, keep proclaiming and keep saying the Word because that is God's Will for how we live our lives.

Invoke God's Word to discover and guide your own unique life's mission.
Do not give up on your petitions, to be shown your God-led destiny.
Be sure to record your Word seed and refer to it often for continued inspiration.

My thoughts:

_____
_____
_____
_____

FEBRUARY
DAY 22

We are in a season of giving, not just giving the minimum requirement as Cain did, but giving God our very best. In this season, we rule over the Cain spirit and we walk in the spirit of Abel who brought the appropriate offering and the very best of his harvest. As we give of ourselves, substance and service this year, let's be mindful to give our very best because God gave us His very best, Jesus Christ and used Him as a First Fruit sacrificial offering to harvest us all.

Giving from the heart has a feeling that goes beyond words. Give your best always, based on your sincere heart-power.

My thoughts:

_____

_____

_____

_____

FEBRUARY
DAY 23

Paul charged Timothy: "Preach the Word! and to be ready in season and out of season. [2 Timothy 4:2] Meaning, talk to people about God according to the Word. The Word is God's seed that He uses to bring about change in us, the earth and the entire universe He's created. God spoke through the eagle-eyed Prophet Isaiah and said, "So shall My Word be that goes forth from My mouth. It shall not return to Me void, but it shall accomplish what I please, and it shall prosper in the thing for which I sent it." God's Word is powerful like a double-edged sword that cuts down through to the joints and marrow. As citizens of the Kingdom, we're responsible for taking the Word into our region, city and neighborhoods. We must hold fast the sound of words we hear and live them daily as we do the work of an evangelist to fulfill our ministry. Be ever more fulfilled in living out the mandate of your life!

Develop the courage to share God with those whom you feel are receptive to receive His Light.
We're of the Source and are a one-world family. We help minister to each other as our needs arise.

My thoughts:

_____
_____
_____
_____

FEBRUARY
DAY 24

In 1 Chronicles 4:10, we see Jabez praying to the Lord to, "keep him from evil, that he would not cause pain." That's because evil vices lurk around us, constantly. Jabez set a pattern in praying for protection. Jesus picked this up in the model prayer: "And do not lead us into temptation but, deliver us from the evil one." [Matthew 6:13] It's significant that even Jesus prayed to stay clear of all evil. We must recognize we're constantly in the presence of evil. Our nature is to sin, so we have the proclivity as Christians to return to sin or darkness as we walk out our destiny in Christ. Therefore, we must intercede daily for God's divine intervention for physical and spiritual salvation because the enemy of our souls is out to kill, steal and destroy us.

A practical tip is to pray for protection before leaving the sanctity of your home.
At work, pray for a friendly and cooperative team spirit to bless all your projects.
Back home, pray for your family to love and serve each other in His Image.

My thoughts:

_____

_____

_____

_____

FEBRUARY
DAY 25

Let us take heed: "For all that is in the world the lust of the flesh, the lust of the eyes, and the pride of life is not of the Father but is of the world." [1 John 2:15] Every believer must be mindful of them as we journey out, day after day. Examples of things that we must be aware of are: 1) Technology; though it can be positive, it also has downsides such as texting, TV and Internet pornography. As Paul would say, "Lawful unto me but they are not expedient for me." 2) Gateways to temptation such as: loneliness and the inability to forgive. When we evaluate these things we must look at them with our spiritual heart to see if they hold more weight in our lives than God. For instance, if you've texted more than you've flipped through the Bible or written to God, then "Houston we got a problem!" If you watched more TV on your flat screen than spending time in prayer, "Houston, something is wrong." We must regulate and moderate our lives so there's a balance in glorifying God. Paul said: "No temptation has overtaken you except such as is common to man; but God is faithful, who will not allow you to be tempted beyond what you are able, but with temptation will also make the way of escape, that you may be able to bear it." [1 Corinthians 10:13] God will always give you an escape route. Follow His lead and live on your petitions until they come to pass. Speak to your mountain with authority with the Word so you can experience Kingdom results. Beware of Temptation Island!

Don't be embarrassed to offer up your temptations to God for Him to transform them.
Admit your limitations and cry for His Word to transform, protect and guide you constantly.

My thoughts:

_____
_____
_____
_____

FEBRUARY
DAY 26

The Bible is very clear in the book of Proverbs, Chapter 3 that we're to: "Honor the Lord with our possessions and with the First Fruits of all your increase." Solomon wrote this out of a pure heart for his followers, so they'd be in a position to receive God's astounding blessings in their lives. Today, we follow this biblical pattern of First Fruit-giving based on this principle. Paul said, "For if the First Fruit is Holy, the lump is also Holy, and if the root is holy, so are the branches." [Romans 11:16] Paul understood this principle, so he laid it out before those for whom he was responsible. In both cases, and as Kingdom citizens, we are to take out of the whole of our possessions a discriminate portion as a First Fruit sacrifice, so that what remains will be Holy and blessed. This then sanctifies everything about us to be blessed because our roots are blessed, along with our branches. God Himself practiced this, too. He had established in the Old Testament, and as a principle in the New Testament, when He gave His only begotten Son to let Him walk in the flesh on earth as a part of humanity. He then took His best or the chief part (Jesus) out of humanity (lump) as a First Fruit offering, so that the lump would be blessed (us). Selflessly pursue the First Fruit Blessing in all your offerings.

Always offer to God your choicest and happiest intentions to satisfy and fulfill Him, in His Way.
Then only will your efforts and possessions become blessed as First Fruits of the highest order.

My thoughts:

_____

_____

_____

_____

FEBRUARY
DAY 27

Learn to be an affectionate giver in the Kingom of God. Affectionate Giving is the highest order of Kingdom giving we must aspire to. This gold standard requires preparation: preparing the mind with scriptural understanding, preparing the heart for sacrificing unselfishly and preparing the hands to sow unwaveringly. Sowing and reaping remains to be the order of God for Kingdom citizens that they would experience great increase. In Genesis, Chapter 8, God made a covenant with creation. He said in Verse 22: "While the earth remains, seed time and harvest, cold and heat, winter and summer, and day and night shall not cease." The power of affectionate giving is a tremendous offering to God because it's symbolic of honoring God in the highest. David brought an extraordinary gift unto the Lord, of special gold and silver treasures. [1 Chronicles 29:3,4,5] This giving was contagious and inspired his congregation to follow his example. David was concerned about the work of the Kingdom as well as the posterity of his people. He gave— knowing that God would cause a supernatural supply in the Kingdom, and as well, release entitlements of the first fruit blessings to Him.

God is generous and unstinting with His blessings.
Let us recognize and honor His largesse with our efforts in giving our best, too.

My thoughts:

_____
_____
_____
_____

FEBRUARY
DAY 28

This year promises to be a phenomenal year, if we but have faith. It will be a year of fruitfulness for the believer. The church shall reap a greater harvest as we sow unto the Kingdom of God. God will allow us to live optimized lives when we become the maximized givers that He desires. "Maximized Givers" are people who understand that their relationship with the Lord has to be mutually beneficial. God wants to release Himself through the believer so that the believer can be a blessing on the earth to manifest Him. Remember when He told Abram in Genesis 12:2,3: "He would bless him, and that he would be a blessing, and that all the families in him of the earth would be blessed?" God is looking for this type of superior partnership. But we must see ourselves as maximizers instead of just good church people. Maximizers are people who choose to face life and operate on spiritual principles of faith with unwavering fortitude to walk in God's best. They live fruitful lives so that they're fulfilled. Maximized givers are Christians who give of their self, substance and service because they understand that if God is going to use them to fulfill Him, then this relationship has to be mutually beneficial and very special.

Our lives mutually benefit each another. Why should it be any different in our relationship with God?
Understand too, that fruitful living arrives at God's own time—not according to our human expectations.
Patience is indeed a divine virtue worth cultivating for fruitful living.

My thoughts:

_____

_____

_____

_____

MARCH
DAY 1

We must get a spiritual perspective on living a maximized life so we don't continue to walk in the old mindset of Christendom. If we're honest, we admit we fall too often on the "give me" mentality. We want God to give us everything we ask for, and usually this list is long. We want a husband, wife, new job, money, vacation, peace of mind, breaking away from illegal drugs; and the list goes on and on. Instead, let's heed Paul: "We must renew our minds and be transformed." [Romans 12:2] Giving selflessly consummates my partnership with God. All believers must mature above and beyond any desire for self-gain to the point where we're solidly anchored to *want* to serve Him without expecting any gain. That's how we become "Maximized Givers" in the Kingdom of God, by establishing trust in Him. When God trusts you, and you trust Him, this becomes an important turning point. Remember Hannah who was barren? She heard and obeyed God by giving her first child back to God. This became her turning point whereby she went on to reap a great harvest of children later in her life. "Allow that your seed can cause a supernatural overflow of blessings to be released into your life—that you won't have room enough to receive it. This is your testing point. And try me now in this, says the Lord." [Malachi 3:10]

Recall the first time you gave over your absolute trust in God to Him.
What happened?
How will you continue living in trust and obedience to God without expecting anything back?

My thoughts:

_____

_____

_____

_____

MARCH
DAY 2

God wants you to be blessed! You hear people say, "Count your blessings" or, "I received a wonderful blessing." Being blessed means: empowered to prosper and succeed by the Grace of God. In Deuteronomy 28:2-13, multiple examples abound with God's blessings if we but obey Him. God always wants to bless His people, in His word. God proclaims: "I pleasure in the prosperity of my people." [Psalm 35:27] Ultimately, when people make these statements, they know God is empowering them to prosper and to succeed. There are no limits to God's largesse. In 2 Peter 1:3, it's noted that God is large and in charge. He sent His Son that we might have, "Life and live more abundantly." When we obey God and apply His principles, we're able to receive those promises laid upon us as Kingdom citizens. God has made an oath with us that He would, "establish us as a Holy people." [Deuteronomy 28:9]

Always proceed with divine confidence in receiving God's Blessings.
Open your heart and meditate on receptivity to more properly receive His Word and boundless gifts.
This is the simple secret of secrets of how to prosper and succeed according to God's Will.

My thoughts:

_____

_____

_____

_____

MARCH
DAY 3

As soldiers in the army of the Lord, we walk in divine authority on earth. We've been chosen to establish the rule and reign of God on the earthly realm. From the very beginning of time God said, "Be fruitful and multiply, and fill the earth and subdue it; have dominion over the fish of the sea, over the birds of the air, and over every living thing that moves on the earth." [Genesis 1:26] God's original intent is for us to exercise the authority He gives us. In the New Testament, Christian Mark commands: "Go into all the world and preach the gospel to every creature. And these signs and wonders will follow them that believe. In My Name they will cast out demons, they will speak with new tongues, they will lay hands on the sick and they will recover." [16:15-18] God desires us to walk in His power to wreak havoc against darkness. Matthew 16:19 announces: "I give you the keys of the Kingdom of heaven and whatever you bind on earth will be bound in heaven, and whatever you loose on earth will be loosed in heaven." Bravely walk in your God-given authority! It's the only way to defeat Satan and darkness throughout the earthly realm.

As God's soldiers spreading His Light, we must believe totally in our God-given authority.
Use this divine authority to overcome every discouraging limitation or obstacle on your journey.
Bravely walk as God's chosen Kingdom citizen to spread His Word fearlessly.

My thoughts:

_____

_____

_____

_____

MARCH
DAY 4

God promises us First Fruit giving produces Seven Blessings: 1) Flow of abundance; 2) Removing the enemy's desire to hurt us; 3) Expanding our land holdings; 4) Driving out oppositions to our increase; 5) His blessings upon our households; 6) Blessing the rest of our increases; 7) For a supernatural supply in the Kingdom of God. [Exodus 23:19-31] But the enemy of your soul will attack in three unholy ways. First, "The Fear of Lordship" is Satan's way of distorting Christian thinking in asking, 'Is this really going to work?' Overcome it with your faith in God. [Romans 12:1,2] Second, Paul spoke about "The Flesh Lordship" in Romans 8:5-8: "Those who live according to the flesh set their minds on the things of the flesh, but those who live according to the spirit, the things of the spirit." Third, "The Flawed Look Lordship" makes Christians look incorrectly at the word; which Paul described in Colossians 2:8: "Beware lest anyone cheat you through philosophy and empty deceit according to tradition of men, according to the basic principles of the world and not according to Christ." Don't let anyone mess up your theology and beliefs. These three groundless fears must be faced—to stay consistent in God's Kingdom!

Memorize God's Seven Blessings to strengthen your resolution in serving Him selflessly.
Cast out the three groundless fears to strengthen your faith in Him as you go about daily living.

My thoughts:

_____

_____

_____

_____

MARCH
DAY 5

As "Kingdom Maximizers" we must always be mindful we're only stewards of what God has given us. Stewards manage the business of others. Believers dutifully manage whatever God entrusts them with. Therefore, we must become faithful in every area of our lives so God can get Glory and Honor from all that we do. We must have the mindset for the Kingdom of God to advance in my generation; and only advance to the degree that I'm committed. Maximized givers dedicate: self, substance and service that we may see the Kingdom of God advance on the earth. God promises when we give unconditionally, it always comes back manifold to us. "You shall receive a hundred-fold return which is representative to an optimum or maximum return on your giving." [Mark 10:28-30] This is a phenomenal rate of return! We've tried the lottery, different forms of gambling, stock market moves, investing strategies and other financial instruments. But no one has been able to follow through on their guarantees with such huge returns as God does. Why? Because His name and word are the GOLD standard. The Bible says: "He's not a man that should lie, nor the Son of man that He would have to repent." Stretch your faith beyond your need and humbly, gratefully welcome God's overflowing blessings!

Nothing on earth is forever. Only the Kingdom of God is eternal, infinite and immortal.
Stretch your faithful stewardship of His blessings with unconditional giving and rejoicing.
In what ways do you give joyfully and gratefully?

My thoughts:

_____
_____
_____
_____

MARCH
DAY 6

We need to consciously put up a selfless demand and an unconditionally pure offering on our seed word to produce a harvest to receive God's grace and His munificence. As we prepare for God's divine harvest, we must learn to prepare our heads, hearts and hands for the unlimited supplies God releases to every believer. Especially to those who give affectionately to Him. Sacrificial obedience without vain petitions will always move divine action—in activating positive changes in the spiritual realm. As we prepare to bring God the most precious treasures we can ever offer, like the widow at Zarepath who gave her last bit of oil and flour to the man of God as the Lord commanded, God will multiply and release an increase of abundance into our lives. "The bin of flour was not used up, nor did the jar of oil run dry, according to the word of the Lord which He spoke by Elijah." [1 Kings 17:16]

Learn to unconditionally offer your choicest offerings to God.
Never expect anything in return, in terms of human expectations,
as in an eye for an eye.
Instead, open your heart with soulful receptivity to receive
gratefully God's limitless blessings, according to His Will.

My thoughts:

_____

_____

_____

_____

MARCH
DAY 7

Christians should give God their best in everything He allows us to work on. God is the shinning example. "He so loved the world that He gave His only and begotten Son, that whoever would believe on Him would have eternal life." [John 3:16] He gave His very best to us and continues to do so, for our lives to be the richer in Him. When we give of ourselves, our service and our substances (such as finances released to God's Kingdom, to purchase food to feed the hungry, clothing and shelter for those less fortunate) there should never ever be any draw back or poverty mind set that causes us to short God with our limitations and greed. "He is the sower who multiples the seed we have sown." [2 Corinthians 9:10] Don't let the enemy cause you to short change your offerings. Know that God will bless you mentally, physically, financially, materially and most important of all, spiritually. Remember, God pleasures and delights in the prosperity of all His people!

What would you like to offer God from the depths of your heart and soulful existence?
How will you do it?
And expand such action to include offerings from your loved ones, as well?

My thoughts:

_____
_____
_____
_____

Joan Sanders

MARCH
DAY 8

The prosperity of the Lord is about everything in your life that's functioning and operating correctly. "The Lord shall increase you more and more, you and your children." [Psalm 115:14] God wants to perpetually increase every aspect of your life for each of you reading this devotional. No matter what you've been through, God has greater things in store for you, including His promised blessings. As you walk out your destiny, remember these "Hall of Famers of the Faithful." Esther was made queen overnight because of the blessing of God upon her life. When the blessing of the Lord is upon you and you're seeking a mate, God will make a divine connection for you, just as God did for Boaz and Ruth. [Ruth 4:1-13] Joseph was thrown into the pit by his jealous brothers; but the Lord's blessing took him from pit to palace. Because it was God's plan for Joseph to deliver his family (even though they had plotted to kill him), he saved them from famine. Incredibly, although Joseph was sold into slavery, he became governor of Egypt. When the blessings of the Lord are upon you, you move from obscurity to celebrated recognition. Keep seeking God and putting Him first, and He will work His miracles on you. From Promise to Provision!

What aspects of your life need to be healed and nurtured to start enjoying God's prosperity?
In what ways will you offer gratitude to celebrate His blessings that you're enjoying now?

My thoughts:

_____
_____
_____
_____

MARCH
DAY 9

Jesus paid for all human redemption through His death, burial and resurrection, thus giving us a New Covenant "founded on better promises." [Hebrews 8:6] However, the principle of first things still remains. God does not change in His character or principles. He is the same yesterday, today and forever more. God considers first things to be holy and devoted to Him alone. Thus today's and every day's First Fruits have to do with the practice of consecrating our every thought and action to Him. God is the main thing! First Fruits means the first in place, order and rank; the beginning, chief or principle thing. First things always belong to Him, in order to establish the rest. The first is the root, from which the rest is determined. God is our ever steadfast Root.

When was your most recent consecration of First Fruit to God?
What happened?
How did this action inspire and uplift you?

My thoughts:

_____

_____

_____

_____

MARCH
DAY 10

Wealth is not limited to income alone. God's wealth has to do with your whole being living in a wholesome, healthy condition. It means nothing is missing, nothing is broken and nothing is out of order; as in maintaining first things first in proper working condition. It means having the blessings of God listed in Deuteronomy 28:2-13. God declared and made manifest in our lives: peace on all sides, protection, provision, healing, restoration and everything else you can ever imagine! "We went through the fire and water, but You brought us to a place of abundance." [Psalm 66:12] Remember the Lord your God. Remember to thank the Lord your God for His abundance gracing every aspect of your life!

God created goodness in everyone—and for us to share selflessly with others.
How do you volunteer your time to serve God in your neighborhood?
Do you fundraise for your organization with a pure heart?

My thoughts:

_____

_____

_____

_____

MARCH
DAY 11

Our spiritual relationship with our Heavenly Father (through the Holy Spirit) becomes first fruit for every relationship we have on this earth. Because of our spiritual relationship, we can express unconditional love in every earthly relationship; whether it's with husband and wife, brother and sister, parent and child, friend, neighbor, co-worker and others. Because of this principle, our relationships are now holy and blessed. The Principle of First Fruits is an important key to abundant living. It can be applied to your time, possessions, job, mind, gifts and talents, words and other areas of your life. Be motivated today to take inventory of your life. Determine who's getting the first fruits in every area of your life. Is it God or the world? If you've not applied spiritual first fruits before, make changes today. Now is the time to take hold of this spiritual principle, put it into action and let the blessings flow! "For if the first fruit is holy, the lump is also holy; and if the root is holy, so are the branches." [Romans 11:16]

Serve and give of your best in all you aspire to and do. What goes around comes around.
Gratefully offering First Fruits is the key for abundance to flow in every area of your life.

My thoughts:

_____

_____

_____

_____

MARCH
DAY 12

Cain worshiped God according to what he thought was enough. His worship had a "form of godliness" but was denied "the power thereof." In other words, it looked good, but Cain failed to tap into the power of blessing without a complete and total faith in God. God gave Cain the opportunity to follow the pattern of what was right. It was the pattern demonstrated by his brother Abel whose First Fruit offering was given in full faith. We must become a giver like David when he brought to the House of the Lord an offering of gold and silver that was meant for the work of the ministry. No one should ever be apprehensive about giving fully of their substance to God. Walk in faith to establish this principle—to experience overflow and an abundance of good things in our lives, for our loved ones and in our surroundings.

It's always fashionable to reflect on God's bountiful goodness.
What lovely surprises have you received recently (that you were not consciously seeking)?
Always remember to give soulful thanks.

My thoughts:

_____

_____

_____

_____

MARCH
DAY 13

Jesus said, "From the days of John the Baptist until now, the Kingdom of Heaven has been forcefully advancing, and forceful men lay hold of it." Since then, an invasion has been under way. A military takeover is constantly in progress; one that no one knows about—except those who have been captured by the enemy. Have you been taken over by the enemy? Instead, allow the Kingdom of Heaven to take over your new life: heart, mind, soul, body, and entire future. Let this divine invasion take over your attitude and make you a dangerous person to the kingdom of darkness. The Kingdom of Heaven is advancing forcefully, and we who are citizens of this Higher Kingdom is part of an "advance force" that must continue to storm the enemy's stronghold. That's because we have a greater power living in us than any other power controlling the world. Jesus said, "In this world you will have trouble. But take heart! I have overcome the world." [Matthew 11:12]

How do you invite good thoughts and intentions into daily living?
Especially when dark forces of depression, suspicion and hostility attack?

My thoughts:

_____

_____

_____

_____

MARCH
DAY 14

God's unmerited favor is available to all humankind. Not because of our goodness, but because of God's goodness and how He wants His plan for our lives to come to pass. In spite of ourselves and our limitations, God's Will must be done. The Bible speaks of Noah being perfect or blameless. Noah found grace in the eyes of the Lord. This is the genealogy of Noah. Noah was a just man, perfect in his generations. Noah walked with God. [Genesis 6:8-9] "And he said unto me, My grace is sufficient for thee: for my strength is made perfect in weakness. Most gladly therefore will I rather glory in my infirmities, that the power of Christ may rest upon me." [2 Corinthians 12:9]

Noah was not perfect and not without sin, like any human being. But he was perfect in that he lived upright and had a close relationship with God.
Will you walk upright before God and obtain the favors that only God can grant?

My thoughts:

_____
_____
_____
_____

MARCH
DAY 15

Confidence and trust are vital ingredients necessary for daily living. Trust involves taking risks. It's the fabric, or glue, that establishes lasting relationships. In life, you've to learn to trust people in many different situations. But even greater and more profound is learning to trust God and knowing He always keeps His word—the highest level of trust to cultivate. The great thing about God is: He's not like us. Trusting Him is an on-purpose and conscious act. When you trust Him, you don't have to worry about anything or what anybody else is doing. Your trust in God will anchor you in tough times, comfort you when people disappoint you and strengthen you when you need it the most. God says, "Trust in Me." And you can certainly take Him at His word!

Children have implicit faith in their parents to care for them and to not let them down.
As children of God, we must constantly share in, and show, this strength of faith in Him.

My thoughts:

_____

_____

_____

_____

MARCH
DAY 16

We are all a part of God's family. There are untold benefits to being in the family of God including: grace, wisdom, power and mercy. "Therefore you are no longer a slave but a son, and if a son, then an heir of God through Christ." [Galatians 4:7] Show your goodness to others in heartfelt ways that are meaningful and joyful for everyone. Celebrate God in yourself and others!

Value your gift of life from God.
Value the lives of others in our great and good family of God.

My thoughts:

_____

_____

_____

_____

MARCH
DAY 17

In taking possession of the land that God gives us, we must go with the mindset that it belongs to us collectively. We must become accountable to one another to sustain the process of enabling us to make a long-term impact in our neighborhoods, cities and regionally. It's of utmost importance to identify critical issues and concerns that may weaken, hinder or threaten our ongoing growth of the ministry. Then, we must take our vision and strategic plan to position us to attract all the vital spiritual resources necessary to pursue projects before us. Numbers 33:50-54 encourages us to know what these are, especially when God gives us a plan. When He gives us the plan, no one, including the enemy, can stop us as long as we follow His instructions. Be Positioned to Possess!

Identify crucial areas in your neighborhood that need improvements. Block watch? Then step up to organize and lead teams in keeping your homes and property safe.
Identify how your ministry efforts relate to neighborhood issues. Are people going hungry? Start a soup kitchen dishing out love, comfort and community sustenance.
Do kids need help with homework? Attention and caring concern? How can you assist?

My thoughts:

_____
_____
_____
_____

MARCH
DAY 18

Biblical fasting is not just a one-shot deal where we suck it up physically and only get really serious with God for a couple of days. It must be part of a total lifestyle obeying God and loving others. If we fast with the right motives, God releases amazing benefits when we submit ourselves to this spiritual discipline. 1) Your light shall break forth like the morning. 2) Your healing shall spring forth speedily. 3) Your righteousness shall go before you. 4) The glory of the Lord shall be your rear guard. 5) You shall call, and the Lord will answer; you shall cry, and He will say, "Here I am." 6) Your light shall dawn in the darkness, and your darkness shall be as the noonday. 7) The Lord will guide you continually, and satisfy your soul in drought, and strengthen your bones. 8) You shall be like a watered garden, and like a spring of water, whose waters do not fail. 9) You shall build the old waste places; you shall raise up the foundations of many generations; and you shall be called the Repairer of the Breach, the Restorer of Streets, to dwell in. When you fast properly according to the Word of God, God is always ready to reward you. [Isaiah 58:8-12]

How to fast properly? Always pray first, confessing your sins and asking the Holy Spirit to lead your life.
Fast with an attitude of humility and with the proper motives.
Meditate on the Word of God.
Seek guidance from your church Elders and officials.
Be sure of proper steps to take, to make it a wholesome and purifying experience.

My thoughts:

_____

_____

_____

_____

MARCH
DAY 19

"Let us operate in the Spirit of Liberality." Even as we dare and want to believe in God, we've been talking about how God wants us to give unto Him. Three ways we give unto the Lord are with: self, substance and service. Even though we may be going through tough times, God doesn't want us to hold back in any way with our selfless acts of giving. In fact, God said: "There is one who scatters yet increases more; and there is one who withholds more than is right, but it leads to poverty." [Proverbs 11:24] Those who are stingy or selfish will become broke; but those who will scatter themselves and their resources will increase. Believers must learn to walk in the spirit of generosity. This is a matter of purpose, principle and prosperity for us as we trust the Lord, even in troubling times. Consciously seek the wisdom of God on how generous He wants us to be. Freely and gratefully you receive, freely you give and live in prosperity!

Do you consider yourself generous—not only with money—but also with time and caring concern for those less fortunate, in spending quality time with them?
Do you volunteer your time helping others with: babysitting, running errands or yard work?

My thoughts:

_____

_____

_____

_____

MARCH
DAY 20

Spiritual warfare consists of battling against evil forces in our minds. The Bible is clear this isn't a battle fought on a physical battle ground. Instead, it's a spiritual battle. We have to be prepared and ready when Satan launches his fiery darts. These darts can be in the form of temptations, deceptions or accusations. We must be prepared with the spiritual arsenal of prayer, praise and the Word that God has equipped us with. The Bible says the weapons of our spiritual warfare are not carnal; but mighty in God. [2 Corinthians 10:4] Wisely use your weapons to defeat Satan. "For we wrestle not against flesh and blood, but against principalities, against powers, against the rulers of the darkness of this world, against spiritual wickedness in high places." [Ephesians 6:12] "Above all, taking the shield of faith, wherewith ye shall be able to quench all the fiery darts of the wicked." [Ephesians 6:16]

Fighting the enemy is a spiritual state of mind—against temptation, deception or accusation.
Be a divine hero who overcomes the enemy by constantly invoking God's grace, protection and guidance.

My thoughts:

_____

_____

_____

_____

MARCH
DAY 21

My prayer is for everyone to have a "God first" mentality. David declared in Psalm 63:1: "Oh God, You are my God; Early will I seek you." The believer must put God first, for God to participate and support their actions throughout the day. Proverb 3:6 advises: "In all your ways acknowledge Him, and He shall direct your paths." 1 Kings 4:29-34 describes the unparalleled wisdom of Solomon, which excelled the wisdom of all men in the East and all the wisdom of Egypt. God gave him wisdom and great understanding so he could speak about trees and animals and every living thing that moved on the earth. His wisdom surpassed that of all men. We should desire to have the wisdom of Solomon if we're going to see prosperous God results each day.

When was the last time you put God first?
What happened?
Record these events; be sure to read them regularly for inspiration and whenever you need to be reassured of His greatness that's guiding your life for eternity.

My thoughts:

_____

_____

_____

_____

MARCH
DAY 22

Spiritual warfare is a battle raging on in our minds between error and truth. If we can know the truth and focus on it, while at the same time ignoring the error, we will be successful in spiritual warfare. Don't let the enemy remind you of past failures and sins. The Bible says we're overcomers. [1 John 4:4] In 2 Corinthians 10:3-5, we're told to cast down imaginations. These are things we imagine that the devil plants in our minds that don't have anything to do with your salvation or healing. Don't listen to anything that opposes the knowledge of God. Just throw it out of your mind and remind the devil who you belong to—to God and overcome the world! Although we walk in the flesh, we don't war after the flesh: "For the weapons of our warfare are not carnal, but mighty through God to the pulling down of strongholds; Casting down imaginations, and every high thing that exalteth itself against the knowledge of God, and bringing into captivity every thought to the obedience of Christ." [2 Corinthians 10:3-5]

Battling the enemy is battling mind over unsound imaginations that can destroy us, if we cave in.
Have faith that God is in charge; give your life over to Him in total confidence that He only wants better for you!

My thoughts:

_____

_____

_____

_____

MARCH
DAY 23

Make some noise. One thing that needs to be better understood within the Body of Christ is the Power of Christ. In many cases, the church needs to understand this as much as the world needs to. Christ is not a weak, impotent, unresponsive force. Our God is a God of power. He impacts every situation and circumstance that He's allowed to enter with revolutionary, life-changing results. One Christian can chase a thousand; two can chase ten thousand when God allows it to be so. The Church bears all the power necessary to heal marriages and to heal those who are sick physically, emotionally, mentally and spiritually. The Church can impact every community, from families to economy. When Jesus came to a city, the magistrates and all city leaders knew it. He worked in such a way that everybody knew He was there. He changed things. It's time for more of us to be noisier about our almighty and powerful Christ! To become dynamic movers and shakers who bravely go into the enemy's camp to take back what was stolen from us.

Do you feel lost in any situation, from relationships to workplace productivity?
The cure is simple. Cry like a child for Christ to show you the way to heal and recover your bearings.

My thoughts:

_____
_____
_____
_____

MARCH
DAY 24

Will you live again? This is an appropriate question for the Body of Christ to ponder. Jesus said to Martha after the death of her brother: "I am the resurrection and the life. He who believes in Me, though he may die, shall live." [John 11: 21-27] No matter what's going on in your life, know that nothing is ever impossible for the Lord to help raise your consciousness and your situation. Jesus spoke to Martha to shift her focus from the death of her brother to the possibility of a miracle. He simply said: "Your brother will rise again." We must know that God can very easily raise us up, in any seemingly impossible and hopeless situation. He can raise us up, from out of sickness, out of debt, out of a bad marriage, out of grief, even out of suicidal hopelessness. He can raise you from whatever struggles you're going through—if you'll only believe in Him and ask Him for help.

What are you feeling hopeless about today?
Then offer your feelings to Christ and cry like a child for Him to uplift you according to His Will.
And have faith in carrying out seemingly impossible odds to overcome your situation.

My thoughts:

_____

_____

_____

_____

MARCH
DAY 25

The Word of God is profitable to Christians in many ways and will help you in your walk with Christ. The Word of God will complete you and equip you for every good work. If you desire to know how to walk in righteousness and to know God and his ways better, begin by reading the Bible; it contains the wisdom you need to live and love your life. If you struggle with reading the Bible, pray God to give you a hunger and thirst for his Word, to help you understand and apply what you read to every practical situation. "But you must continue in the things which you have learned and been assured of, knowing from whom you have learned them." [2 Timothy 3:14-17]

Being the "Good Book," the Bible offers extraordinary insights to the most ordinary situations.
It's time well spent every day—to read, reread and understand even just one passage.

My thoughts:

_____

_____

_____

_____

MARCH
DAY 26

To be a Kingdom citizen is to make sure that your foundation is solid and proven. If you secure your salvation with the Word of God, you'll be able to withstand any storm. [Matthew 7:24-25] "He is like a man building a house who dug down deep and laid the foundation on rock. When a flood came, the torrent struck that house but could not shake it, because it was well built." [Luke 6:48]

Your solid faith in God is the only thing that matters.
Dig deep to solidly build up a rock-solid foundation of faith that's capable of weathering storms.

My thoughts:

_____

_____

_____

_____

MARCH
DAY 27

"The good man brings good things out of the good stored up in his heart, and the evil man brings evil things out of the evil stored up in his heart. For out of the overflow of his heart his mouth speaks." [Luke 6:45] Listen carefully to a person's words, for they reveal his heart. We try to portray what we want other people to see. Some people are transparent. Others are very guarded and private. But our mouths will eventually show what's hidden within, and reveal the true nature of our hearts. Listen carefully and you'll be able to tell what the person has stored up inside—and whether he or she is committed to God or committed to their own interests.

Listen carefully with your heart's wisdom, wisdom solidly anchored in Christ's Word.
Open your heart only to those who sincerely care for you, not just anyone with ulterior motives.

My thoughts:

_____
_____
_____
_____

MARCH
DAY 28

Spiritual gifts are intended to be used in service to others. [1 Peter 4:10] To "serve" is the word from which we get "deacon." The Greek word for spiritual gift is "charisma." The word for "grace" is, "charis." When we show charisma to another, we're distributing God's grace. As you come to know which spiritual gifts you're blessed with, recognize that they're not to be used for individual selfish desires. When you use them as they're divinely intended, you become God's servant, and He'll work through you to pour out grace on His people. Whatever strengths we have, come from God; whatever abilities we have, come from God. Speak the utterances of God. Serve with pure intentions and the ability will be supplied by God. While spiritual gifts are to edify and build up the body of Christ, this is not the ultimate goal. The ultimate goal is to glorify God. If we're able to accomplish anything through working with our spiritual gifts, remember that God is the One who gets the glory. "That in all things God may be glorified through Jesus Christ, to Whom belong the glory and the dominion forever and ever. Amen." [1 Peter 4:11]

All that we are as parents or professionals, in aspiring to the highest, come from God's grace.
Remember to offer soulful gratitude at every step of the way to glorify His working in and through us.

My thoughts:

_____
_____
_____
_____

MARCH
DAY 29

Jesus intended for the disciples to produce His likeness in and through the church, while being gathered out around the world. Thus His ministry in the Spirit would be duplicated manifold by His ministry through the lives of His disciples and others like them. His ministry would continue expanding in ever enlarging circumference until the multitudes would know the opportunities the disciples had known with the Lord. Jesus intends for us to be about in the world, with the same strategy, to win souls for Him as we live out our lives in Him. Ask: How many people have been affected by the ministry I show?

When was the last time you mentioned Christ in your conversations with others?
Think of innovative ways to gently slip in a good word about Him with people you feel good about and are comfortable with. This is a more effective strategy than engaging in verbal combat with unbelievers and hostile folks.

My thoughts:

_____
_____
_____
_____

MARCH
DAY 30

The resurrection of Jesus Christ from the dead is the central fact of Christian history. The Church is built on this heavenly phenomenon; without it, there would be no Christian Church today. Jesus' Resurrection is unique. Other religions have strong ethical systems, concepts about paradise and various holy scriptures. Christianity is privileged to have God's Son, who became man, then literally died for His people—and was raised again in power and glory to rule His Church forever. Amen!

As we celebrate the Resurrection this Easter, let us not forget how privileged we are to be in constant contact with our Lord God, through Jesus Christ, His Son.
As a Kingdom citizen, how do you honor this extra special event with family and friends?

My thoughts:

_____

_____

_____

_____

MARCH
DAY 31

The author of Acts 17:28 declared: "For in Him we live and move and have our being." We are the very offsprings of God." Genesis 1:26 proclaimed: "We were made in His image, according to His likeness." And because we are representatives of Him and modeled after Him, we're spirit-led beings living the human experience. Paul said, "For as many as are led by the Spirit of God, these are the sons of God." [Romans 8:14] Simply put, if we obey Him and walk according to His Will, we have a son or daughter relationship with our Heavenly Father. When we're divinely and intimately connected, the Bible points out: "In Him we live, and move, and have our being." God blesses us with life. We are His children. God wants to bless His people, as we continue to remain faithful unto Him.

Human parents have the highest hopes for their children. So does God.
We're even more privileged because God forgives us in season and out, unlike some people.
Do you find it easy to forgive and forget in your heart, and to move on positively?

My thoughts:

_____

_____

_____

_____

April
Day 1

Faith is not just believing in it and claiming it. Living a life of faith is a powerful and enriching lifestyle based on quality choices and decisions. What you do daily affects your faith, and vice versa. Therefore, just believing is not enough. There's something else. In making choices, we forsake something old to acquire something new. To forsake means to leave something behind. True faith forsakes old, redundant beliefs and dysfunctional rituals. Faith forsakes old ways and embraces the new that God is constantly offering us. "By faith Moses forsook Egypt, not fearing the wrath of the King." [Hebrews 11:27] Why did Moses forsake Egypt? Because nothing will happen until he left behind old habits—to embrace new ones. Nothing will happen until you decide to forsake the old ways you used to do things, to wholeheartedly acquire new ways of looking at the world and in doing things with, and for, God. God said: "Behold, I will do a new thing, now it shall spring forth. Shall you not know it?" [Isaiah 43:19]

To make progress with our lives, we have to continuously question whether we're using old tools that are no longer relevant or useful.
Learn to unlearn the old, so you become more adept in learning newer ways of living happier, healthier and more fulfilling lives. God is a great example because He's constantly transcending Himself with new, progressive ways.

My thoughts:

_____

_____

_____

_____

APRIL
DAY 2

The next level of a deeper faith gets God's attention. In Mark, Chapter 2, Jesus healed and forgave the man who had a paralytic condition—thanks to the faith of four of his committed friends. The men who brought their palsied friend to Jesus were true men of faith. They had an active, enlivened, relentless faith in Jesus. They had faith in action. These men were not ordinary believers. They were radical. They weren't about to let anything get in the way of their receiving from Jesus. They wanted to get a blessing and weren't going home until they got it. When you go to church, make a commitment that you aren't going to go home until you've received from God what you need, and want to receive, from Him. Say to yourself, "I'm not going home until I come out of the bondage I'm in, until I'm delivered from the pressures I feel. I'm not going home until I get the blessing I need. I'm not going home until I release the unforgiveness, discouragement, anger or resentment I feel." Each of us must open up and draw out every bit of the power of Christ that's in us to stay the course with deep faith. Draw out the power of Christ in the singing, preaching, teaching, worship, giving and praying. Put your faith to action and expect to receive according to His Will!

Healthiness is next to godliness.
Release all your hurt, anger, resentment and negative emotions.
Cast them out of your system!
It'll be easier to heal—to faithfully receive God's forgiveness for yourself and others.

My thoughts:

_____
_____
_____
_____

APRIL
DAY 3

What is man that you are mindful of him? First and foremost, God is our Creator. "Let us make man in Our image, according to Our likeness." [Genesis 1:26] He was intentional in creating us as human beings to be like Him and to make us lower than the angels crowned with glory and honor. Second, we're created with purpose. Dr. Myles Munroe said, "If you do not understand the purpose of a thing, you will abuse it." Purpose gives you meaning for living a spiritual life in God. Before you were a twinkle in your parent's eyes, God had predestined you for greatness and called you with a holy calling. Third, He gave us, male and female, equal dominion and authority because He's a God of equality and desires for us to be stewards over His earth.

Although God created each person to be unique, God created man and woman to be equal in His Likeness.
We're created to uphold the stewardship He's entrusted us with the goal to purposefully live meaningful lives in and for Him.

My thoughts:

_____

_____

_____

_____

APRIL
DAY 4

We're living in critical times requiring critical solutions. Our economy is fractured, with people jobless, homeless and living in survival mode. The disparities we're experiencing with our education, health and justice systems are alarming. As believers, we must seek the face of God for the problems of the world, our region, community at large and our personal circumstances. We must be ever vigilant in our times of consecration and prayer interceding on behalf of ourselves, others, world issues and these perilous times. As we penetrate this darkness with prayer and intercession, expect catastrophic change to appear in our homes, neighborhoods, workplaces, relationships, economy and in our personal lives. This type of prayer is transformational and will cause heavenly results to be manifested on earth. "The Kingdom come, Thy will be done on earth, as it is in heaven." [Matthew 6:10]

Our heartfelt, intense prayers are powerful in moving God to intercede on behalf of our and the world's perilous problems. This type of prayer is transformational—be prepared to receive and manifest His grace.

My thoughts:

_____
_____
_____
_____

APRIL
DAY 5

We're at the threshold of something powerful. Ask the Holy Spirit to come, lead and guide you throughout this day. As you do this, He'll direct you in the ways of truth and righteousness. Today, please be intentional about bombarding the heavens with prayers that will cause a fresh encounter with God. Fervently pray that God will hear you and transform your life. God is able to change a people, a church, a region and a nation based on the power of our words. The effective, fervent prayer of a righteous man avails much. [James 5:16]

No fervent, sincere prayers will go unheeded by God.
When we cry out to God, even as a child, He will hear us and be moved to intercede on our behalf.
And have faith in God's transformational impact on your life—however unexpected they may be.

My thoughts:

_____

_____

_____

_____

APRIL
DAY 6

Each of us has a responsibility to bear the Light of the Lord. Paul said that we live in a "crooked and perverse generation, among who we ought to shine as lights in the world." [Philippians 2:15] Our lives ought to shine forth God's Light because He works us according to His Will for His good pleasure. He enables us to be the light not by might, but by His spirit. Thus, we must work out our soul's salvation to always make progress in our faith. We can hear all of the sermons we want. We can attend as many Bible studies as we want. We can talk about God all we want, but at the end of the day, we must work out our own soul's salvation. Nobody can do this for us. Sometimes, we're our own worst enemy. We allow ourselves to be stunted because of the enemy inside. Paul said, "For you were once darkness, but now you are light in the Lord. Walk as children of light." Jesus said, "You are the light of the world, a city that is set on a hill cannot be hidden." [Matthew 5:14] No matter where you are, whatever you're doing, the light of the Lord shines through you continuously. Hold up up that Light before a watching world to inspire others!

As Kingdom citizens ablaze with the Light of the Lord, we must proudly shine forth our light everywhere.
No one can do this for us—except ourselves, by our own soul's willpower to want to share His Light around the world.

My thoughts:

_____

_____

_____

_____

APRIL
DAY 7

You have the potential for greater. Potential is hidden capacity, untapped power and unreleased energy. It's all you could be, but haven't yet become. "Now unto Him who is able to exceedingly abundantly above all that we ask or think, according to the power or potential that works in us." [Ephesians 3:20] The mighty power of God's spirit walking inside of you is enabling you to fulfill your mission. Potential is determined by the assignment that God has given you. Recognize that whatever you were born to do, you were equipped to do it—and well. God releases resources to you as you need to get the job done. Three men were given the talents in Matthew 25 and were equipped with the resources they needed to fulfill their assignments. God put the Holy Spirit in us, with more than enough potential for our needs. The power worked within two of the men who put their talents to good use and gained more. But one of the servants chose to hide his potential, His divine resource. We must be like the two men who realized the potential for increase that had been placed in their hands. "To whom much is given, much is required; to whom much is committed, of him they will ask the more." [Luke 12:48]

Never underestimate the powerful potential God has blessed each and every one of us with!
We only have to: 1) recognize this power by way of persistent striving to manifest and offer our very best; and 2) consciously seek our edge to manifest these talents in whatever leadership, creative, athletic or other pursuits we're called upon to honor and to serve.

My thoughts:

_____
_____
_____
_____

APRIL
DAY 8

God desires to have a relationship with you. He wants to know that you're committed to him and have made a decision to follow his Word and Way for your life. Revelation 2:4 encourages us to return back to God. Recommit your life to Him today. Commitment to God means you're making God your highest priority. We also must strive to be rooted and grounded in the Word of God. David announced: "Your word I have hidden in my heart." [Psalm 119:11] Read the word and meditate on it daily, that we may come to know the richness of God's love for us.

Our relationship with God is our most sacred mission to uphold and love in life.
Commit and consecrate your life to walk in God with total devotion and trust.

My thoughts:

_____

_____

_____

_____

APRIL
DAY 9

Humility is a foundational characteristic for every believer to possess. The Bible encourages us in to have the mind of Christ. [Philippians 2:1-5] Through these scriptures, we learn to walk in unity with our fellow brothers and sisters, in the gospel. We ought to be selfless in our dealings with others and with humility, esteem others better than ourselves and have concern for their wellbeing.

Humility is not about showing a person's low self-esteem.
Humility is about showing selfless concern for the well-being of others—with kindness, sweetness, gentleness, forgiveness and affection.

My thoughts:

_____

_____

_____

_____

APRIL
DAY 10

Walking in the Spirit will lead to a transformed life. To walk in the spirit is to follow the lead in allowing Him to teach you, guide you and transform your mind, body and heart. If you walk in the Spirit, you won't carry out desires of the flesh. [Galatians 5:16] A spirit-minded person displays the fruits of love, joy, peace, long suffering tolerance, goodness, kindness, gentleness, faithfulness and self-control. [Galatians 5:22-23] As you serve and offer these fruitful concerns, you'll experience the power of God in your life. You can live a life of faith knowing that you're pleasing God in His own way.

Walking in His Spirit leads to an unimaginably transformed life enriched by His grace.
Selflessly offering your wealth to others also nurtures richness in extraordinary ways.

My thoughts:

_____
_____
_____
_____

APRIL
DAY 11

God has already divinely set up for us to live a triumphant life in Him. Paul said: "Thanks be to God who always leads us in triumph in Christ." [2 Corinthians 2:14] As Christians, we always win when we walk with the Lord, and when our lives line up in Him. To stay on track we must eagerly run, with a deep-seated determination and lifelong endurance, the exciting race that has been set before us. We must not get weary while walking and running. In due season, you shall reap the rewards of your generous and self-giving efforts.

Give thanks for the triumphant life God has laid out for us as Kingdom citizens.
We humbly play our roles with our soul's determination, to not give up on our glorious life journeys, no matter what the conditions may be.

My thoughts:

_____

_____

_____

_____

APRIL
DAY 12

To successfully walk in the Spirit, we must submit ourselves emotionally, physically, socially and intellectually unto His Will. We must learn to gradually give up the desires of the flesh to participate in the divine grace of God. [Galatians 5:24-25] It's similar to coming clean from addictions—such as smoking. Commit to gradually lessening your intake to cleanse your senses, as trying to stop cold-turkey may not prove fruitful. Forgive your past negligence and habits. For those who are Christ's own have crucified the flesh with its passions and desires. As we live in the Spirit, let us also walk in the Spirit.

What do you need to do, to change and transform your life gloriously?
Are you nailing your sins to the cross?
Has the Holy Spirit become the source of your new life and practical lifestyle—in staying happy, healthy and engaged while spreading the gospel?

My thoughts:

_____
_____
_____
_____

APRIL
DAY 13

When a catastrophic or traumatic situation arises in your life, remember that God answers prayers. "Lord, it is nothing for You to help, whether with many or with those who have no power; help us, O Lord our God, for we rest on You, and in Your name we go against this multitude. O Lord, You are our God; do not let man prevail against You!" [2 Chronicles 14:11] Amazing things can happen when you choose to pray. Instead of taking matters into your own hands or resorting to violence or neglect, prayer should be your first line of defense in every situation.

Better still; heed how an ounce of prevention saves pounds of cure later.
Start committing now to a soulful and dedicated prayer life—for His protection and guidance to better lead your life more safely, healthily and happily.
Begin with a few minutes of daily prayers. As you take periodic breaks throughout the day to rebalance your energy levels, revitalize with prayer breaks to rebalance your spiritual life, too.

My thoughts:

_____

_____

_____

_____

APRIL
DAY 14

This is your day to shine for the Lord. Jesus said: "Follow Me, and I will make you become fishers of men." [Mark 1:17] In following Jesus, we should be catching souls for the Kingdom of God. God will make you an attractive magnet, a Holy Ghost fishing net, to see the unsaved come in. He will work on you to become a prophetic evangelist. You don't have to get there on your own. Jesus said, "Follow Me." In other words, He's setting the example, so follow His example. Jesus' mission is for His life to be reproduced in us, that we would model our ministry after Him. Signs from Heaven furnish us with prophetic fuel so we have the courage and spiritual energy to rise up, then reap the harvest, regardless of world conditions. It's so important to know what the season is. In God's Kingdom, His reign is not ruled by calendars and clocks, but by seasons. We're in a unique season today. There are many church leaders entering into 21-day fasts and many people giving themselves over to 24-hour prayer campaigns, healing rooms, and concerts of prayers. You don't sow like that without gaining a monumental reaping. It's time to harvest; time to pray; time to fast; and time to get out there spiritually. He's moving us into a new season to realize our heavenly worth with today's spirited activities.

How would you like to shine forth your light with your activities? To become a fisher of men inspiring others to see God's light in themselves, too?

My thoughts:

_____

_____

_____

_____

APRIL
DAY 15

We have been commissioned by God to spread the gospel. When you're commissioned, you're sent and authorized to perform a mission. Paul says: "But you shall receive power after that the Holy Ghost is come upon you, and you shall be witnesses unto me both in Jerusalem and in all Judea, and in Samaria and unto the uttermost parts of the world." [Acts 1:8] There's no shortage of souls to be drawn into the Kingdom of God. We all know someone who either does not know about salvation that comes from the Lord, or who knew, but for some reason hasn't been able to maintain a lifestyle of sanctification. As you carry out the mission that God has given you to either plant the seed of salvation or water it, The Lord himself will give increase to your evangelism efforts. For Jesus said, the harvest truly is plentiful, but the laborers are few. Will you be a laborer in God's vineyard today, and moving on?

Kingdom citizens are divinely charged to spread God's message to help others find His peace.
Many are waiting to be informed and nurtured to receive the gospels; they'll be grateful in turn to keep paying it forward by telling many more about God's salvation for them.

My thoughts:

_____

_____

_____

_____

APRIL
DAY 16

God commits to those who are faithful. "Therefore, my Son, be strong in the grace that is in Christ Jesus. And the things that you have heard from me among many witnesses, commit these to faithful men who will be able to teach others also." [2 Timothy 2:1-5] To be faithful means to exhibit: consistency, loyalty, ability to sticking with vision, reliability and trustworthiness. God gives to every man according to his ability. He demonstrated this in Matthew 25 by giving three servants with clear differences in their abilities to produce different amounts of talents: one five, one two and the other, one talent. You have what you have because God has surveyed your life and seen how much you can handle. He's given you just enough to demonstrate to Him that He can trust you with more. God rewards the faithful and doesn't allow us to be barren. He gives freely and justly to all. Don't make excuses for being unproductive in the Kingdom of God. Excuses rely on temporary conditions and prohibit you from receiving permanent results. When you're unfaithful, it causes God to raise up your replacement, and for others to have to compensate by stepping in to get the job done. Learn to live a faithful life by being productive. Who can find a faithful man? [Proverbs 20:6] Faithful people are rare, but we can be faithful by following the example of Jesus who was faithful until his death.

The beauty of committing to God results in limitless blessings for you.
Give unconditionally, step up to the plate and faithfully serve God according to the talents He's blessed you with.

My thoughts:

_____

_____

_____

_____

APRIL
DAY 17

Jesus said in Luke 19:13: "And He called His ten servants, and delivered them ten pounds, and said unto them, 'Occupy till I come.'" The word occupy is a military term. To occupy something doesn't mean to just sit in the pew of a church. Instead, an occupational force is strategically put in place to fight enemies. After the war is won, the occupational force remains, so pockets of resistance can be extinguished. God has put you on earth as an occupational force. We're given the authority on this planet to rise up and fight pockets of spiritual resistance that come against God's intentions. The war has already been won on Calvary. It's over! But the story continues in us, because the Bibles states God is going to crush Satan underneath our feet. [Romans 16:20] To occupy also means to do business. We've got to step up, to do the Father's business. The Father's business is about redemption and saving souls; it's a supernatural business. God demands this so He would be represented by more than mere words—but by our heroic determination to win the war against the forces of darkness.

We can start to occupy our Father's business by first dealing with enemies of resistance from within us—fear, insecurity, doubt, jealousy, suspicion and other negative qualities. When we lighten up with less baggage, we're on firmer ground to win the war! Onward!

My thoughts:

_____

_____

_____

_____

APRIL
DAY 18

God is not a philosophy; He is not a concept. God is the real force of the entire universe. He is the force behind all we are, and do. God is saying that what is required to be a witness in this hour is: we must lead a dunamis lifestyle and not just pay lip service to it. This is a lifestyle of unimaginable power and divine authority. We have to march forward to share His Light with others!

God is unfathomable—close and intimate though He is with, and in, us.
But He's seeded us with faith and divine surrender to doing His Will.
Prayer and meditation on His infinite blessings will bear fruit to show us our life's mission.

My thoughts:

_____
_____
_____
_____

APRIL
DAY 19

Triumphant Living! This is a powerful phrase for the Body of Christ because God wants to use us to manifest Him. And the world is looking for us to show them how. As believers, we must be responsible in dealing with spiritual enemies. Paul shared with us that our spiritual enemies are principalities, powers, rulers of this world and wickedness in high places. [Ephesians 6:12] He was very clear they weren't our family, friends or peers; but the enemy after our souls. We must gird up with the appropiate gear of God to triumph over the enemy. Paul also said something intriguing: "We wrestle." Meaning, the enemy and us are in close proximty to each other. We're on guard and ready to attack by taking advantage of each other's weak points. The enemy seeks to devour by attacking our emotions, thoughts, decision-making skills and the physical body. We must war daily against these hostile forces to experience victory and triumph as God has planned for us. That's how we become victorious—from living triumphant lives over the enemy!

Be ever vigilant about how the enemy or hostile forces attack our emotions, thoughts and actions.
Become a triumphant hero warrior on the battlefield of life—by manifesting God's Light diligently against these negative forces of mass destruction.

My thoughts:

_____
_____
_____
_____

APRIL
DAY 20

Today, we take control of our thought life and bring every thought to the Will and Word of God. Be careful not to compare yourself to anyone else, because comparing yourself to someone else can lead to discontentment. Understand that you're precious in the sight of God. He loves you for your uniqueness, gifts and talents. "When they measure themselves with themselves and compare themselves with one another, they are without understanding and behave unwisely." [2 Corinthians 10:12] When faced with a situation where you're tempted to compare yourself to someone else, look to Jesus Christ, who is our ultimate example for all things good

It's pointless to compare ourselves with others as God has created each of us uniquely.
Just be grateful for opportunities to manifest the precious gifts He's blessed you with.

My thoughts:

_____

_____

_____

_____

APRIL
DAY 21

Things don't just happen haphazardly when you have a life plan that manifests the Kingdom of God. You can prepare for great success in your life with this plan, according to His Will. "Where there is no vision, the people perish: but he that keepeth the law, happy is he." [Proverbs 29:18] Develop a vision for your family to look at where you've been and where you plan to go, to move forward productively. Pray hard to discover how to manifest and fulfill specific tactics to successfully move your strategy, in how you're going to get to where you'd like to be, for now and for the future. "A man's heart plans his way, But the Lord directs his steps." [Proverbs 16:9]

Ask God: What's my life's mission; and for my family?
Ask God: How to develop a strategy with specific tactics to achieve the goals You have for us?

My thoughts:

_____
_____
_____
_____

APRIL
DAY 22

Is the nature of a fallen man to hide from God? Adam tried to hide from God. But how ridiculous it is to think we can hide from Him! Our Creator's omniscience supersedes our frail ability to be deceptive. Adam confessed, after he was pressed by his Father, "I heard your voice in the garden, and I was afraid, because I was naked; and I hid myself." [Genesis. 3:10] Do you see what the first man did? He hid himself. No wonder we're lost. We've hidden ourselves. We didn't hide our work or our gifts; instead, we have hidden ourselves from God. When we hide from God, we lose. What good is it to know where everything is, if we cannot find our true selves? Our loss causes a desperation that produces sin and separation. Like the prodigal son in Luke Chapter 15, we need to come to our senses and emerge from under the bushes. We need to become transparent in the presence of the Lord. If Adam had only run toward, instead of away, from God, he could have been delivered! Don't hide!

When you make a mistake, don't try to hide or disavow it. Fess up and invoke God's protection.
God is everywhere and all where, so He knows. Just be like a brave child crying out for your Father's forgiveness. His love will definitely make you whole again.

My thoughts:

_____
_____
_____
_____

APRIL
DAY 23

Jesus said, "Behold, a sower went out to sow. And he sowed, some seed fell by the wayside; and the birds came and devoured them. Some fell on stony places, where they did not have much earth; and they immediately sprang up because they had no depth of earth. But when the sun was up they were scorched, and because they had no root they withered away. And some fell among thorns, and the thorns sprang up and choked them. But others fell on good ground and yielded a crop; some a hundredfold, some sixty, some thirty." [Matthew 13:3-9] God's word impacts people differently. Falling by "the wayside" on hardened surfaces, a seed won't sprout. That's when the word bounces off shallow people who feel great on Sunday, wave their hands or dance at church; but live an undisciplined, ungodly life. They may believe they're "saved," but are wasting God's time at church. They haven't allowed the seed to settle, take root and grow in them. The seed that falls among thorns means the word of God is heard by people so wrapped up with workaholic or addictive habits, they've never experienced a complete cleansing from the past. Physically or emotionally, they can't, won't or don't need to let go of attachments, and wonder why they're not achieving greater things and why God's Word isn't working for them. The seed that falls on good ground shows a person who hears, understands and applies the Word of God to their life— where a cultivated growth of the word is producing a bountiful harvest.

What kind of seed would you like to sow, to serve God better? How will you manifest God's gifts in you to help and benefit others? Joyfully count the ways!

My thoughts:

_____

_____

_____

_____

APRIL
DAY 24

The promise that God has made to His people comes with a generational focus. And behold, the word of the Lord came to him, saying, "This one shall not be your heir, but one who will come from your own body shall be your heir." Then He brought him outside and said, "Look now toward heaven, and count the stars if you are able to number them." And He said to him, "So shall your descendants be." And he believed in the Lord, and He accounted it to him for righteousness. [Genesis 15:4-6] Abraham knew that nations would be blessed through him. "And give the blessing of Abraham to you and your descendants with you, that you may inherit the land in which you are a stranger, Which God gave to Abraham." [Genesis 28:4] As Jesus was counseling the rich young ruler, He encouraged the young ruler to obey the laws and commandments. When asked how to inherit eternal life, Jesus lovingly responded that he must sell all of his possessions and give the proceeds to the poor.

What are you willing to give up, to follow Jesus?
More specifically, giving up bad and unwholesome habits that hinder your spiritual progress?

My thoughts:

_____

_____

_____

_____

APRIL
DAY 25

Scripture says we have the ability to bind and loose. [Matthew 16:18,19] As soldiers in the army of the most High God, we must stand up high to shut down the enemy. Jesus said, "The gates of hell would not prevail against us," so we must walk in our God-given authority and power to stand our ground against the enemy. The power to bind and loose is a spiritual authority that is given to the children of God. Understand that we've been given keys to the Kingdom; we have keys to unlock the blessings of God to be released over the course of our lives. In Luke 12:42, the master of the house gave the steward keys to the storehouse where provisions were kept, so he'd give to everyone in the house their portion of meat in due season. When we bind, we constrict the enemy's actions that are intended to harm us. When we loosen up, we open the flow of spirit to move on our behalf. John said, "For this purpose the Son of God was manifested, that He might destroy the works of the devil." [1 John 3:8] Remember, it's reassuring to know that our fight is fixed in that we have already won by God's grace. Now, all we have to do is go on our way, with our daily binding and loosing so we maintain powerful control over the enemy.

Always stand tall for your love of God and His manifestations. Let no one disavow you from your fixed and glorious victories in working for God.

My thoughts:

_____
_____
_____
_____

APRIL
DAY 26

Surround yourself today with men and women who are of like mind with you and will help and support you as you walk out the plan and purpose that God has for you and them. Expose, reveal and remove anything that is not right according to the Word of God. "Do not be yoked together with unbelievers. For what do righteousness and wickedness have in common? Or what fellowship can light have with darkness?" [2 Corinthians 6:14]

Socialize with like-minded friends who support and walk with you in God's Plan.
Disassociate from those who pull you down with their disbeliefs and unhealthy ways.

My thoughts:

_____

_____

_____

_____

APRIL
DAY 27

Take courage and follow the example of Queen Esther. [Esther, Chapter 4] Be proud of who you are and be willing to stand up to take action. Recognize your position of influence and don't be afraid to step up to the plate. King Ahasuerus was convinced to write a decree to murder all the Jews of that land because they didn't keep the King's laws. Distressed by this decree, Mordecai approached Queen Esther to intercede to the King on behalf of herself and her people. Queen Esther found the courage to approach the King (which was against the law since she had not been asked to the King's chamber). After praying and fasting, she asked for the King's help, even if it meant death for herself.

Follow your soul's indomitable courage to speak for, and act on, righteousness in God.
Purify and fortify your mission first, to properly know and do God's Will.

My thoughts:

_____

_____

_____

_____

APRIL
DAY 28

"So God created man in his own image, in the image of God He created them; male and female, He created them." [Genesis 1:27] Adam was created for a specific purpose, to rule and exert dominion over the earth and everything on it. [Genesis 1:26] Eve was also created for a specific purpose, to also have dominion over the earth and to be a helper to Adam. You also have a specific purpose for which you're created to divinely fulfill. In Him also we have obtained an inheritance, in being predestined according to the purpose of Him who works all things according to the counsel of His will. [Ephesians 1:11] Be mindful in knowing the purpose of your creation, to better fulfill the purpose that God has you for.

Pray and meditate on your life's mission to better fulfill God. Live your life richly according to His Will, not your individual will.

My thoughts:
_____
_____
_____
_____

APRIL
DAY 29

No matter what we see, do, or have going on in our lives, God always wants us to have better. From the very beginning when He placed Adam in the garden of paradise, His thoughts were for us to have better. Even after Adam sinned and fell, He still desired for us to have better by sending his only begotten Son, Jesus, who was always in agreement with His Father. Remember the man at the pool of Bethesda after he was made well (or better) and Jesus said to him: "See, you have been made better. Sin no more, lest a worse thing come on you." [John 5:14] Don't let anything keep you away from living a life of better in Him. Why settle for worse when you can have, and live better in, Jesus Christ?

Never settle for anything less than your highest aspirations to manifest your God-given destiny.
Make your Father proud in utilizing the skills and talents He's gifted you—whether parent, teacher, carpenter, construction worker, or student.

My thoughts:

_____
_____
_____
_____

APRIL
DAY 30

The writer of Hebrews 6:12 advised: "That you do not become sluggish, but imitate those who through faith and patience inherit the promises." The promises of God are "yea" and "amen." When God makes a promise to us, He follows through, as long as we don't become sluggish or weary in doing well. It's easy to allow ourselves to enter that mode because of how we think. If a promised result doesn't come quickly we forget about it. But if we're sincere about experiencing the supernatural increase God wants to give us, we have to change our way of thinking. Faith is limited by our human expectations. The engine of faith is fueled by our divine expectations. Faith is the substance of things hoped for, the evidence of things not seen. [Hebrews 11:1] This is the expectation. Expectation is expanded through exposure to the grace of God. We're saved by grace through faith. [Ephesians 2:8] Plus, the more we're exposed, the greater our expectations are. Scripture is clear about the abundance that God wants every believer to have and experience. Solomon said: "The blessings of the Lord make one rich, and He adds no sorrow with it." [Proverbs 10:22] It simply means God wants to expand your capacity to do more to manifest Him. And He never asks anyone to do more—without expanding their capacity.

When the going gets tough or sluggish, it's even more imperative to not give up.
Take a break. Pause a while. Pray for Him to inspire you on in His Way, in doing well.

My thoughts:

_____

_____

_____

_____

MAY
DAY 1

God wants to perpetually increase you and your family's precious assets. Such as good health, education, health care, a safe home and of course finances to pay for them. So the key to our inheriting the promises of God is valuing what God's Word says above all others. You must place a priority in listening to the word daily, because it's your life source. What a great example the woman in 1 Kings 17 is! She valued the word even though her situation was dismal. She was down to her last meal with her son. Then she heard the voice of God and gave the Prophet Elijah the first of what she had left. Thereafter she ate well for many days with her son; her flour was never used up nor did her jar of oil run dry. How so? It was all because she valued God's word more than her physical situation. God was moved by her deep-seated faith, and blessed her with perpetual increase to come into her life. Serve the Lord according to His Word and you, too, will experience supernatural increases for life—according to His Will. The word of the Lord says, "May the Lord give you increase more and more to you and your children." [Psalm 115:14]

The value of internal wealth far supersedes external wealth when we place our faith in God's Word.
Whenever you feel down and out, fill your heart with the wealth of assurance that God cares for you and provides everything—if you but ask and listen.

My thoughts:

_____
_____
_____
_____

MAY
DAY 2

Manifest your divine boldness. "And when they had prayed, the place where they were assembled together was shaken; and they were all filled with the Holy Spirit, and they spoke the word of God with boldness." [Acts 4:31] The story is told of Peter and John in Jerusalem, of how their enemies had gathered together against Christ. Being against Christ meant being against the people of God; but Peter and John had one voice and were of one accord. There was one sound that went up to heaven. The disciples' prayer was for God to grace them with the Word, and to not be afraid of the face of man. May God grant us the ability to speak His Word with boldness—even in the face of unwarranted opposition and unfounded threats.

Your divine boldness to speak up and manifest God is inspiring—especially in the face of enemies.
Stay steadfast in your beliefs; pray to always be guided by Him to be on His side.

My thoughts:

_____
_____
_____
_____

MAY
DAY 3

There is power in the Church. Let's establish the fact that you are the church. Paul said in 1 Corinthians 3:16: "Do you know that you are the Temple of God and that the Spirit of God dwells in you." Now let's establish that you have power. And when He had called His twelve disciples to Him, He gave them power over unclean spirits to cast them out, and to heal all kinds of sickness and all kinds of disease. [Matthew 10:1] According to Acts 1:8, we are to release this power in Jerusalem, and in all Judea and Samaria, and to the ends of the earth. You're empowered to do ministry in your home, communities, regionally and all over the world. This power is translated from the Hebrew word "dunamis," which is power, energy, light, might, great force, ability and strength. When you use this power, you're able to transform everything around you. Be like the apostles who performed many signs and wonders among the people. The believers used to meet together in Solomon's Colonnade. No one else dared join them, even though they were highly regarded by the people. Nevertheless, more and more men and women believed in the Lord and were added to their numbers. As a result, people brought the sick into the streets and laid them on beds and mats so that at least Peter's shadow might fall on some of them as he passed by. Crowds gathered also from towns around Jerusalem, bringing their sick and those tormented by impure spirits; all were healed. [Acts 5:12-16]

God's power is in every one.
Honor this mighty power of the Lord and release it by serving at home and everywhere you are.
Honor your ministry to selflessly serve in His Will and power.

My thoughts:

_____

_____

_____

_____

MAY
DAY 4

To maintain our citizenship in the Kingdom of God, we must show Him we love Him by keeping His commandments. Jesus said, "He that hath My commandments, and keepeth them, he it is that loveth Me: and he that loveth Me shall be loved of My Father, and I will love him, and will manifest Myself to him." [John 14:21] For our relationship to be right with God, we must love Him unconditionally, in whatever situation we find ourselves in. The Heavenly Father has no greater love at every monment, than for all His children everywhere.

God's love is not like the human carnal lust of binding or conditional giving and taking.
God's love is pure unconditional affection, untainted by earthly demands.
Loving and serving God in His Word is the only passport anyone ever needs to get to Heaven.

My thoughts:

_____
_____
_____
_____

MAY
DAY 5

From the moment of His conception, Jesus was anointed by the Holy Spirit. Jesus was always intimate with the Holy Spirit because His very nature was both divine and human. As the Anointed One, Jesus was led, empowered and continually filled with the Holy Spirit. The moment you're born again happens when the nature of Jesus Christ takes birth in you. You become a new creation in Christ. [2 Corinthians 5:17] The Holy Spirit has birthed in you a new divine nature in God. Christ's Spirit lives in you and empowers you to live the Christian Life. Paul declared, "I myself no longer live, but Christ lives in me. So I live my life in this earthly body by trusting in the Son of God, who loved me and gave himself for me. [Galatians 2:20] Like Jesus, you too can live the Spirit-led life because as a believer, you're born of the Holy Spirit. Go out today, be like Jesus and live a holy life like Him!

Living the Spirit-led life is totally practical as we go about our daily activities.
It happens when we: talk kindly and are patient with others, smile from the heart and allow another driver to go first especially if they've an emergency on their hands. These actions are divine and practical, while manifesting the Holy Spirit with our brothers and sisters.

My thoughts:

_____
_____
_____
_____

MAY
DAY 6

Hebrews 11:4 talks about Abel giving a "more excellent" sacrifice than Cain. Abel and Cain both had gotten a word by faith from the Lord for their sacrificial giving in worship. However Cain (elder of the two) decided to give God something less than was required. The Bible says Cain "brought the fruit of the ground," suggesting he brought God just any old thing as a way to worship Him. When you worship God you can't just bring Him any old thing. True worship is focused on God and not the worshipper. True worship requires you give and not expect to receive anything in return. Jesus said, "It is more blessed to give than to receive" [Acts 20:35] and "give and it shall be given unto you. [Luke 6:38]" True worship emanates from the Spirit of a person, springing forth from the intellect, emotions and willpower. Jesus told the woman at the well, "But the hour is coming and now is, when the true worshippers will worship the Father in spirit and truth; for the Father is seeking such to worship Him. God is a spirit, and those who worship Him must worship in spirit and truth." [John 4:24] Now is the hour to give God our true, pure worship in raising the bar from substandard worship to the highest level of excellence. Excellence means superior, first class, very good. In worshipping God we must do it in an excellent way. Abel did it by faith, and it was pleasing to the Lord that even to this day, it's a testimony that stands the test of times. No matter what you do, do it with a spirit of excellence!

Honor God in all you do by giving superior service—whether at home, the workplace, while shopping or driving.
Honor God in His Likeness with everyone you meet and interact with, as they're also blessed with the Holy Spirit.

My thoughts:

_____

_____

_____

_____

MAY
DAY 7

As we pursue God in taking steps for better, we *must* want better. God always wants better for believers. "God pleasures in the prosperity of His people." [Psalm 35:27] Jesus said: "I came to give you life and life more better." [John 10:10] In John Chapter 5:2-9, a man wanted better—but according to the world's system which says: relieve stress with cigarettes, forget problems by drinking, or take substances that control your mind. But to the contrary, each of these false admonitions damage us. The man who had been at the pool for 38 years was trying to get better by using the wrong system. Jesus asked him: "Do you want to be made well?" The man gave an excuse, in blaming someone else for not being able to get into the pool. Porch people around him were sick, blind and lame. Porch people represent stagnant places we find ourselves in. These people drain the life out of you, in preventing you from living a passionate life in Christ. That's why we must put our best efforts towards a better quality of life in Him. Paul said: "I do not count myself to have apprehended, but one thing I do forgetting those things that are behind and reaching forward to those things that are ahead." [Philippians 3:13]

Don't let negative lifestyle habits (smoking, drinking or
addiction) attack your good sensibilities.
Use common sense to discern unwholesome false promises;
instead, consciously strive to live a wholesome God-blessed life.

My thoughts:

_____
_____
_____
_____

MAY
DAY 8

Proverb 4:20 exhorts us to pursue the Kingdom of God with passion, and to give the Word of God our full attention. "Faith comes by hearing and hearing the word of God." [Romans 10:17] "God is a rewarder of those who diligently seek Him." [Hebrews 11:6] You need to hotly pursue God sincerely, with pure intentions to experience Him better. After Jesus got into the head of the man and pulled him away from the porch people, the man became ready to receive Christ for better. Jesus told him, "Rise, take up your bed and walk." Immediately, the man was made better. If you want God to do anything to help you, you must begin to rise above your circumstances—no matter what it looks like at that time. When we let go of our small controlling ego, God can then step in immediately, to turn our situation around, and cause us to do the impossible!

It's tough to let go, in order to let God take the lead with our lives, isn't it?
Unconditional surrender to the Master means giving God our full attention, and to offer everything we have and confront, for His transformation-grace to smooth out our lives.

My thoughts:

_____

_____

_____

_____

MAY
DAY 9

Maintaining your spiritual love life is vital. "But you, beloved, building yourselves up on your most holy faith, praying in the Holy Spirit, keep yourselves in the love of God, looking for the mercy of our Lord Jesus Christ unto eternal life." [Jude 1:20-21] This is a very personal message that Jude is delivering. In building ourselves up, on our most Holy faith, we should use faith as a foundation. He suggests that if you're going to maintain your love for God, you'll need to build yourself up in what you've been taught in the scriptures. We're taught the truth and the Word of God that was once and for all entrusted to the saints. To keep ourselves in the love of God, as believers, we must be occupied with God's love and strive to be in fellowship with Him. "As the Father loved me, I also have loved you; abide in my love." [John 15:9] Abide in the love of God.

God's message is all about love—pure, unconditional love of self, others, animals, flora and fauna and the entire galaxy He created.
With love, we can live peacefully and amicably.
When we're at peace with ourselves, we invite prosperity into our lives.

My thoughts:

_____
_____
_____
_____

MAY
DAY 10

David said, "O how love I thy law! it is my meditation all the day." If we are to maintain our citizenship in God we must love God's law and keep it close to our hearts. Loving God's law requires we obey Him and meditate on His word daily. When we meditate on the Word of God, David said we shall be "like trees planted by the rivers of water, that bringeth forth his fruit in his season; his leaf also shall not wither; and whatsoever he doeth shall prosper." [Psalm 1:3]

Every day offer thanks for the opportunity to wake up loving God and living His law.
Heartfelt invocations are always heard by Him to forgive our misguided actions.
By offering our past failures and mistakes to Him, we'll be purified to receive better, thanks to His never-ending love for all.

My thoughts:

_____

_____

_____

_____

MAY
DAY 11

As you embark upon this day, I'm hopeful it'll be "Purpose Driven." Solomon said: "Many are the plans in a man's heart, but it is the Lord's purpose that prevails." As we journey through this day, it's important to know God's Purpose for your life. For example, when Jesus was concluding His last day of ministry with His disciples, He washed their feet. He told them: "Now that you know these things, you will be blessed if you do them." Once you know what God wants you to do, the blessing comes in actually doing it, without any expectation of worldly gain.

Start each day with a prayerful cry for the Lord's Purpose to fill your heart and in guiding your every action.
Meditate soulfully for 5-10 minutes on what your day's amazing purpose is, according to His Word. God's Purpose for us changes daily, so tune in anew each day.
Never falter. Keep these flashes of divine inspiration in your heart and mind to inspire you throughout the day.

My thoughts:

_____

_____

_____

_____

MAY
DAY 12

The key to a healthy church starts with you. On the day of Pentecost, the Spirit of the Lord unified us as one church. The product of fellowship is unity, which requires we be intentional in relating to our brothers and sisters in the Lord. Unity pleases God. "How good and pleasant it is for brethren to dwell together in unity." [Psalm 133] In order for us to see healthy spiritual growth in the Kingdom, we must relate to one another no matter what our past experiences have been, prior to our being saved by the Holy Spirit. As we go about our day, God has positioned us strategically in places where we need to be, to carry out His work (job, neighborhood, family, marketplace). We must relate with caring concern and kindness with those we come in contact, so their souls would be won unto Him. Dig a little deeper while relating to those whom God has connected you to, in your local congregation. Spend quality time with them. Go out to breakfast, lunch, dinner and invite them over for coffee or tea. Pray that you seek God on how to expand the Kingdom for healthy results with everyone you come in contact with.

You'll be amazed and delighted how friendly folks are when you reach out to them.
In our conscious fellowship with one another, we joyfully manifest the Lord and please Him much.

My thoughts:

_____

_____

_____

_____

MAY
DAY 13

God rebirths through every believer. Major events will cause the world to stand up and divinely recognize the Kingdom of God. In Luke 1:26, we see God sent the messenger Gabriel to speak prophetically into the life of Mary for her major moment. Mary was very taken aback. The Bible says she was "afraid." Mary had frailties just like all of us. But God was still faithful to His promise. Now, God won't send a major message to just anyone—only to those who have become pure in heart and spirit. Only those who are sanctified, purified and separated unto the Lord for God's good works will be sent major messages. In fact, if we're going to see signs and wonders as well, we've to let the Lord come into our lives with our pure hearts and spirits. Only then can He release His Glory for our good. After God has entered your life, you have to conceive it, in order for it to manifest. When Mary conceived in her spirit, it gave God the green light to cause a major moment in the earthly realm through Mary. Thus was born The Son, Christ Himself. God wants to birth something major through you, too. All you have to do is get in the birthing position for Him to do it. Incredibly, you're positively pregnant with promise!

We're all candidates for God's Word to manifest in us according to His Will.
Always end every prayer with: "Thy Will Be Done."
Then, no matter the major or minor event, you release
apprehension and doubt, so His word is fulfilled in and through
you.

My thoughts:

_____
_____
_____
_____

MAY
DAY 14

From Luke 19:13 the word of the day is: "Occupy Until He Comes." The word occupy means to do business; and as well, a military term meaning, "advance and hold." Jesus challenged the disciples and people of that day on their belief that the Kingdom would appear immediately. But that was not the case! Jesus had said to them the process would be: He would die first, sit at the right hand of the Father and then return to continue His Father's work. But in the meantime, while He's away, we must continue to do business and manifest the Kingdom of God.

As Kingdom citizens, never give up believing and trying to manifest the Lord.
Your honest intentions are well-known to God because He is omniscient and all-knowing.

My thoughts:

_____
_____
_____
_____

MAY
DAY 15

Forgiveness is not easy because our emotions and feelings can cause us to be so caught up that we justify ourselves to continue walking in unforgiveness. Jesus said: "Forgive men their trespasses and you shall be forgiven." [Matthew 6:15] Let us be intentional in forgiving, and as well, learn to overcome our emotions and feelings that can put us in situations of great danger. As believers, we want to walk in a heartfelt place where we know without the shadow of a doubt that our relationship with God is right on, and that He hears us constantly. So, learn to let go of whatever negative or hurtful emotions you're holding on to, to become free and released from baggage that stifles the next move God has for your momentous life.

Learn to unlearn the old, so you'll be filled with newness and healing joy.
It's true we have to unlearn the old (forsake them!) in order to learn the new.
God is a real gentleman who helps us forgive and forget—so we may walk right on, in Him!

My thoughts:
_____
_____
_____
_____

MAY
DAY 16

The object of our faith is God and His Word. The goal of attaining faith is to never ever fear fear, as we walk in His Word. The more we know about God and His word, the more faith we have. The less we know, the smaller is our shield and the easier it'll be for one of Satan's fiery darts to reach its target. The simple secret to growing a larger protective shield of faith is to increase your knowledge of God and His word. "So then faith comes by hearing, and hearing by the word of God." [Romans 10:17]

Life is a constant battlefield in facing never-ending challenges.
Never give in to fear—aka "false evidence appearing real."
But the protective armor of faith always saves the day.
To grow a larger, more protective armor, simply increase your
faith in God's protection grace.

My thoughts:

_____

_____

_____

_____

MAY
DAY 17

"The Lord Has Need of You." [Luke 19:30,31] For those of us who have been slack in serving the Lord, don't give up yet. He's calling you now to switch out the old, and go the opposite of how you haven't been engaged in kingdom work. He specifically gave two disciples instructions on where to go, to do the work of the Lord. This is the time for us to begin doing things differently, to get different results. These men were part of a prophetic movement of God. Every man and every beast have to play their respective roles. It was prophesized Jesus would ride on a colt for His triumphal re-entry into Jerusalem. Symbolically, the colt, the foal of a donkey, was used to usher in divine victory, salvation and peace. [Zechariah 9:9]

It's never too late to invite God into our lives.
Never too late either to take up divine arms to further His (our) ministry.
What attracts you to expanding our ministry, and in what ways?

My thoughts:
_____
_____
_____
_____

MAY
DAY 18

We are called by the love of God. Jesus said: "For God so loved the world that He gave his only and begotten son that whoever believes Him should not perish but have everlasting life." [John 3:16] Being called is to be summoned. The "called" is also a royal priesthood, a holy nation, His own special people who proclaim His praises. Paul said: "For by grace you have been saved through faith and that not of yourselves; it is the gift of God." [Ephesians 2:8] As the called, we must allow the Holy Spirit to lead us. Paul said for as many as are led by the Spirit of God these are sons of God. The Spirit will lead you, guide you, comfort you and teach you how to live victoriously. The ultimate benefit to living in the spirit is eternal life. He who sows to the spirit shall reap eternal life and he who sows to the flesh shall reap corruption. [Galatians 6:8] To be "called-out citizens" of the Kingdom that God is looking for, we must go through a change. And for change to take place, we must renew our minds. Paul said: "Do not be conformed to this world, But be transformed by the renewing of your mind that you may prove what is the good and acceptable and perfect will of God." [Romans 12:2]

Be unafraid to change your old ways, to attain ongoing new states of perfection.
Kingdom citizens are privileged to be called out to honor and live in the Holy Spirit.

My thoughts:

_____
_____
_____
_____

MAY
DAY 19

Fifty days after the ascension of Jesus Christ, the day of Pentecost came like a mighty rushing windstorm to fill believers so they'd be enabled to do supernatural things. "And they were all filled with the Holy Spirit and began to speak with other tongues, as the Spirit gave them utterance." [Acts 2:4] We're still experiencing the phenomenal outpouring of the Holy Spirit, still dwelling within us and still desiring to empower us to do great exploits for the Lord. As Charismatic Christians, we've been given grace gifts for the profit of all. Tongues were given to every believer who accepted Him into their lives. Everyone may not speak in their spiritual language but that doesn't mean it doesn't exist. Tongues are meant for Personal Edification [1 Corinthians 14:2-4] and Public Exhortation [1 Corinthians 14:12-15]. We must know when to use them in proper order and place. For those not using the gift of tongues, seek the Lord for them and believe God for the weapon of tongues so you're able to pray in the spirit. For those who already have it, continue to use it on a daily basis so your intimacy with God deepens and enriches your wisdom.

The power of speaking in tongues lies in deepening our understanding of God's Word.
Speaking in tongues also enables and empowers us to go beyond the personal into the public realm to share God's Word with others.

My thoughts:

_____

_____

_____

_____

MAY
DAY 20

Each of us who are born-again believers have been empowered to walk in the spirit of excellence. God is *the* excellent God. Scripture says: "How excellent is Your Name in all of the earth." [Psalm 8:1] Since God lives in us we, too, can be excellent. To be excellent means to be: superior, first class, or top of the line. God made us in His image to be superior beings.

Understand that all our ways of living better are always divine gifts of grace.
If you desire quality living and superior amenities, offer your situation to God for His gracious transformation.

My thoughts:

_____

_____

_____

_____

MAY
DAY 21

If we're going to walk in the spirit of excellence for our families, businesses, employers and those God brings to our paths, we need wisdom, the real wisdom from within and not just knowledge. If we feel we lack wisdom, just ask God. The Book of James advises: "Let us ask of God who gives to all liberally." [1:5] It's that simple—all you have to do is ask. No matter what the situation, God gives according to His Will. Please understand that we cannot expect God to give on our terms. Solomon with all his wisdom and excellence enabled people to recognize the God in him. The Queen of Sheba was not connected to God but when she finished meeting with this man of God, all she could say was, "Blessed be the name of your God." Just try to walk in the wisdom and excellence of God, and watch it become contagious to others, too. Then, Give Praise unto God!

Real wisdom of, and in, God is the true wealth of walking in His Word.
The beauty of walking in His Word is that no other words are needed for people to see and feel God working to light up all of your successes.

My thoughts:

_____

_____

_____

_____

MAY
DAY 22

Jesus was neither afraid nor embarrassed to be seen in the company of the poor and the hungry, the sick and the destitute, or to be thought of as, "a friend of tax collectors and sinners." [Luke 7:34] After all, that is why He came to minister to all peoples. "Those who are well have no need of a physician, but those who are sick, do. "I did not come to call the righteous, but sinners, to repentance." [Mark 2:17] We have a mandate from Jesus, by His own words and example, to take care of society's poor and less fortunate citizens.

Research nonprofits and civil agencies in your area catering to the less fortunate.
Then consider which one calls to you as a good fit—spiritually, emotionally and professionally.
Volunteer to serve selflessly, without any expectation of returns.
Who knows, God may increase your capacity to serve in even more amazing ways.

My thoughts:

_____
_____
_____
_____

MAY
DAY 23

There is Power in Oneness. "Therefore a man shall leave his father and mother and be joined to his wife, and they shall become one flesh." [Genesis 2:24] God is the creator of family. He sets the order for family and gives us an example of what family should look like. He created the first family in His image and described them as "one flesh." In Hebrew, "One, Unit, or Unity" describes Him. He is a Triune God (Father, Son and Holy Spirit). Each aspect has a different function, but they're all one in bringing Glory unto Him. He joined man and woman together so they would come together in union, to become "heirs together of His grace" and to bring Him Glory and Honor.

Marriage is sacred. This sacred power of oneness grows, solidifies and strengthens family.
Honor the privilege of your sacred union with your spouse and kids—with total fidelity.

My thoughts:

_____

_____

_____

_____

MAY
DAY 24

It's important to cultivate an ongoing Godly Wisdom in the affairs of daily life. Solomon said: "The Lord stores up sound wisdom for the upright." [Proverb 2:7] As we go about our daily routines, we should seek God for practical wisdom to apply in our daily activities. Solomon pronounced: "Wisdom is the principle thing; Therefore get wisdom, and in all of your getting, get understanding." [Proverbs 4:7] Consciously make wisdom your Principle Thing today and every day, as you occupy and do His business.

Practical wisdom isn't removed from divine wisdom. Applying common sense to all our actions reflects our true wisdom in integrating wealth with the demands of the day's business. Anytime you're flustered or confused in the mind, pause, take a few deep breaths and get centered in your heart again to feel His Presence guiding you on wisely.
The power of your prayerful, heartfelt cries for God's Wisdom to guide you will be heard!

My thoughts:

_____
_____
_____
_____

MAY
DAY 25

The Queen of Sheba [1 Kings 10:1-6] wanted what Solomon had. They were in the same business selling commodities and running fleets of ships to major ports. But Solomon had the upper hand because he was connected to God. His connection caused him to flourish and to far exceed her in every way. She journeyed out to visit with him to find out what he was doing that she wasn't. She realized half of his story had not been told. She was in awe of his wisdom and all that he had built. It wasn't Solomon's natural abilities of course, but his possessing the wisdom of God to do the needful. "Wisdom is the principle thing; therefore get wisdom and in all your getting, get an understanding." [Proverbs 4:7] Solomon had the wisdom of God for his situation and for those he was responsible for leading.

God's wisdom is unparalleled in guiding us to every successful endeavor.
However, we do have to learn to walk with obedience and trust in His Way.

My thoughts:

_____

_____

_____

_____

MAY
DAY 26

"You are a chosen generation, a royal priest hood, a holy nation, His own special people, that you may proclaim the praises of Him who called you out of darkness into His marvelous light; who once were not a people but are now the people of God, who had not obtained mercy but now have obtained mercy." [1 Peter 2:9-10] Today, the Christian Church, particularly in America, is at a crossroads. The challenges of "seeking our brothers" and reaching the lost with the gospel are greater than ever before. Attitudes, methods and programs of the past are no longer adequate. New challenges call for new approaches. The needs of the lost, the needy, the hurting,the rejected and the dying are outpacing the Church's ability to keep up with demands. We can no longer be satisfied to "do church" or "do ministry" in the old ways. We can no longer afford simply to sit inside the four walls of our church building and hope that those who are hurting come to us. Jesus commanded us to go serve others. "God has always raised up in every generation a company of people strategically placed in church and society through whom He can fulfill His purpose and bring His will to pass in the earth. We are our brothers' keepers." [Matthew 28:19,20]

Look around. How can you serve those in need with a pure heart?
Start with family by offering your unbridled love and emotional support.
And keep an eye and an ear out to see where your talents and practical skills might suitably serve your community.

My thoughts:

_____

_____

_____

_____

MAY
DAY 27

In the book of Acts, Jesus gave the disciples their last proclamation regarding the Father and His sending on the Holy Spirit. "But you shall receive power after the Holy Spirit has come upon you." [Acts 1:8] This was a passing of the baton for the Church to continue in the same vein as the Lord's. He has empowered us to be witnesses within our own city, the region other parts of our country and then, ultimately, globally. We've been anointed to expand the Kingdom of God beyond measureless measure. What a divine honor for us to uphold! Each of you have a testimony to tell. Try to approach at least two people who are waiting to be saved this week, to plant seed, or water the seed that's already been sown. Then, believe in God for the increase.

It's easy to say hi to strangers. Just be friendly and they'll open up because everyone loves to tell stories (or testimonies). Before long, you'll intuitively know when and how to connect with them in heartfelt, spiritual ways to plant or water the seed.

My thoughts:

_____

_____

_____

_____

MAY
DAY 28

Jesus was showing himself again to the disciples at the Sea of Galilee. Jesus was dealing with Peter and six other disciples concerning transition and shifting. [John 21:3-6] The disciples had gone back to doing what was comfortable to a few of them, fishing in a boat but had caught nothing. Jesus told them to transition and to shift their nets to the right side of the boat. Their obedience to shift caused them to catch a multitude of fish. Sometimes, what is right in front of us can only be realized when we shift from doing it the old way, to doing right in God's way.

Learn to be flexible and develop the ability to shift attitudes, tactics and ways of doing things to come out ahead.
Divine obedience is another winning quality to develop—from listening to His Word.

My thoughts:

_____
_____
_____
_____

MAY
DAY 29

A key to answered prayer is forgiveness. When we forgive another, we cease to feel resentment against them. We're able to allow room for an error or weakness. God forgives us, all the time. "For if you forgive men their trespasses, your Heavenly Father will also forgive you." [Matthew 6:14] To demonstrate true forgiveness, be a believer. Don't hold grudges. Be willing to forgive another each and every time we're wronged. We must be willing to forgive quickly, too. "Be angry, and do not sin: do not let the sun go down on your wrath." [Ephesians 4:26] When you have a heart ready to forgive and are able to come to an agreement with your adversary, God said He would show up and bring a holy resolve to the issue. "Again I say to you that if two of you agree on earth concerning anything that they ask, it will be done for them by My Father in heaven. For where two or three are gathered together in My name, I am there in the midst of them." [Matthew 18:19]

When we forgive others, an important step is achieved in making more spiritual progress.
How? God himself shows up!

My thoughts:

_____

_____

_____

_____

MAY
DAY 30

Everyone must practice the art of forgiveness. And please understand that in order to forgive others, we must be willing to look at our own ability to hurt, offend and injure those around us. Sadly, they're often people we love the most. However, we discover the Lord's Prayer provides us with a key insight into how we can experience the joy and abundant life that Jesus told us He can bring. "Give us this day our daily bread, and forgive us our trespasses as we forgive those who trespass against us." [Matthew 6:11-12] People don't realize that when they pray this most famous prayer, they themselves are forgiving other people, too. God isn't punishing us this way in telling us we'll receive from Him the same thing we've dished out to others. God is much bigger than that! He's much more loving, gracious and compassionate to us—His children. Jesus reveals in the Lord's Prayer that our human capacity to receive God's grace is blocked when we're not willing to forgive those who have hurt us. We cannot embrace God's forgiveness if we're so busy clinging to past wounds and nursing old grudges. To move into the blessings of our future, we must relinquish the pains of the past.

Forsake the hurtful, unprogressive past. Past is dust!
Forgive and forget in order to move forward—so we continue to
grow in God's Love, Light and Joy.

My thoughts:

_____

_____

_____

_____

MAY
DAY 31

We're all blessed to be a blessing. To be blessed is to be prosperous and successful. It means we have the ability to move forward in doing the things of God. We're blessed because we've been redeemed by the blood of the lamb. What a precious price to pay for our salvation! When Jesus died on the cross, he took the power away from the enemy to kill our souls. Christ has redeemed us from the curse of the law, having become a curse for us (for it is written, "Cursed is everyone who hangs on a tree") that the blessing of Abraham might come upon the Gentiles in Christ Jesus, that we might receive the promise of the Spirit through faith. [Galatians 3:13-14]

You are blessed to be a blessing unto others; so rejoice in your divine honor!
Aspire to inspire others to see their blessings as spiritual beings too, while being challenged to live in a material world.
Your divine example will inspire them to seek God's Way, too.

My thoughts:

_____

_____

_____

_____

JUNE
DAY 1

God is love. The Lord provides many examples of love in the Word of God. He shows us how we are to express love through our obedience to Him. "For this is the love of God, that we keep His commandments. And His commandments are not burdensome." [1 John 5:3] Loving was not designed to be a chore, but a blessing to everyone. God urges us to love one another. "For all the law is fulfilled in one word, even in this: "You shall love your neighbor as yourself." [Galatians 5:14] We are to continually show love to others for the sake of Christ. He loves us unconditionally, regardless of a person's background or social status. [John 3:16] Jesus addressed the disciples, "A new commandment I give to you, that you love one another; as I have loved you, that you also love one another." [John 13:34]

Do you notice and feel the love in your family?
If yes, write down 10 gratitude blessings that bring your family joy.
If not so much, ask: What can we do more, to increase the love in our home?

My thoughts:

_____

_____

_____

_____

JUNE
DAY 2

Each of us have an assignment that we must fulfill in the Holy Spirit. May your efforts to win over those who are ready to receive the Holy Spirit be fruitful. Make the opportunity to minister to many who are looking forward to being healed, delivered, redeemed or saved for the Lord. Remember you have been endowed with power to do great exploits for the Lord. Just stay focused on your spiritual mission to manifest God, so we experience an outpouring of manifestation of the Lord like never before!

Meditate every morning on your day's mission to carry out the Lord's Will.
What gives joy to the person you're interacting with?
It's important to leave each encounter with a smile on both your faces.

My thoughts:

_____

_____

_____

_____

JUNE
DAY 3

God is redefining His Church. He's reorienting us to the mission we've had all along: reaching the masses in our cities with the gospel. Therein lies the future and the hope of the Church. Therein lies the passion of the Church! We should be passionate about our Lord and compassionate towards others, especially those who have lost their spiritual way and need to know that Christ still loves them. Whenever Jesus visited Bethany, He always stayed at the home of Mary and Martha and their brother, Lazarus. At one visit, Martha scurried around trying to be a good hostess while her sister Mary simply sat at Jesus' feet, listening to Him. Martha ministered to Jesus' humanity, seeking to serve His physical needs. Mary, on the other hand, ministered to Jesus by seeking simply to be with Him. [Luke 10:38-42] Martha had compassion for the man Jesus; Mary had passion for the person who was the Son of God. Both are important. The earliest Christians served the needs of others out of compassion that was fueled by their passion for Christ. We are a Vital Church!

In conducting our compassionate ministry, we must attend to both the secular and the spiritual needs of those whom we serve. Integrating compassion with divine passion is a great way to selflessly manifest the Grace of the Lord.

My thoughts:

_____

_____

_____

_____

JUNE
DAY 4

Caleb had attributes of character, confidence and courage that gave him the godlike tenacity to hold on to his faith. Especially when he was in the midst of what looked like being doomed with the worst possible disaster. The secret to Caleb's faith? "If the Lord is pleased with us, then He will bring us into this land and give it to us a land which flows with milk and honey." [Numbers 14:8] He was expressing his confidence in God's integrity. He believed God would bless his people if they would stay true to God's commands: "Only do not rebel against the Lord; and do not fear the people of the land, for they will be our prey. Their protection has been removed from them, and the Lord is with us; do not fear them." [Verse 9] God brought them out of Egypt so He could take them to the Promised Land. There was no need to fear, worry or fret. Fear, doom nor gloom have no place in a believer's life. If you're feeling out of sorts, the simplest and most effective way to recover is to walk in the above attributes. By showing God your loyalty to His word, even in the face of adversity, God will reward you in His own Way. Caleb believed God and made every effort to follow his Word. "Nevertheless my brethren who went up with me made the heart of the people melt with fear; but I followed the Lord my God fully." [Joshua 14:8]

Hang in there with your faith, especially when the going gets tough.
Offer your adversity to God and cry out to Him for His guidance to proceed divinely.

My thoughts:

_____
_____
_____
_____

JUNE
DAY 5

We're often our own worst enemy when it comes to forgiveness. We forgive those who have committed the most heinous offenses against us. Yet, we carry around thousand-pound packs of resentment, anger, frustration and even hatred toward ourselves for our misguided actions. People end up feeling guilty and ashamed for not being able to forgive themselves; thus further complicating this internal drama that can grip us like a deadly vise in squeezing us tighter and tighter—by our own hand, no less! This snare is not only debilitating, but also goes against God's fundamental rule about how we interact with one another. It can be summed up as: "Love thy neighbor as thyself." [Leviticus 19:18] Jesus confirms and aligns Himself with what His Father taught: that all divine laws essentially rely on two fundamentals: Love God with all your heart, soul, mind and strength; and love your neighbor as you love ourself.

First, learn to forgive yourself for every inadvertent mistake and unavoidable failure.
Remember, everyone makes mistakes; and failures are but pillars to building future success.
Love yourself as God loves us, so do no harm to your emotions, mind and body.

My thoughts:

_____

_____

_____

_____

JUNE
DAY 6

God will put you in the place you're meant to occupy if you ask and trust Him for it. This simple request allows you to live in the Holy Spirit, so His glory will always be upon you. If you miss it, take a page from David's request: "Lord, restore to me the joy of your salvation." [Psalm 51:12] If you feel out of touch with God, get back to Calvary and keep near the Cross. Let the God of Glory glorify Himself in and through you as you strive to achieve your highest aspirations.

Often, when we aspire to reach God in the highest, the hostile forces attack us even more vehemently by pulling us down with self-doubt, suspicion and all manner of insecurities.
But keep the faith, cry inwardly and be inspired like David for God to restore your true joy.

My thoughts:

_____

_____

_____

_____

JUNE
DAY 7

All believers have a testimony or story to tell that displays the goodness and mercy of God. Or a story that simply demonstrates that the hand of God is on your life based on a trial, struggle, or dangerous situation that you know only God brought you through. Many believers are afraid, hesitant or embarrassed to tell these stories because they don't understand the spiritual purpose for having to travel down that road on their spiritual journey. The reason is to glorify God. Every believer, no matter at what age or stage of your Christian walk, must be able to not only forgive, but be forgiven of past failures or situations that you've felt hindered your walk with God. It's time to forgive yourself. Forgiving oneself is important to every Christian and provides a key to spiritual breakthrough. "Confess your trespasses to one another, and pray for one another, that you may be healed. The effective, fervent prayer of a righteous man avails much." [James 5:16] It's cleansing, revealing, refreshing and reviving. To forgive oneself is to allow one's spirit to arise anew, like a phoenix emerging from the ashes in overcoming a setback that had seemed insurmountable.

When was the most seemingly deplorable situation you had to face? What did you do to work through it?
How did the end results show that it was God's unseen hand lovingly guiding you through a deep, healing experience?

My thoughts:

_____

_____

_____

_____

JUNE
DAY 8

In Ephesians 4:11-16, Paul penned an epistle to the churches, as he was stirred by the Holy Spirit. He placed a strong emphasis on growing spiritually to a mature level and reaching unity with those in the faith. [Verse 14] This is a must for every believer for the rest of the body and Kingdom citizens to grow into. There are non-spiritual practices that must cease as we make progress towards divine maturity. The childish and irresponsible nature is done away with. As mature saints, our ears are tuned in to the frequency of God. We will be able to hear, know and speak the truth of God in His love and guidance. What you spiritually do daily does affect the spiritual growth of your brothers and sisters, too—be they on our path or on another.

Reflect on how you'd like to manifest God's Light with your Kingdom brothers and sisters.
Would you like to be seen as gracious, generous and compassionate?
As they say, action speaks louder than words.

My thoughts:

_____

_____

_____

_____

JUNE
DAY 9

Your spirituality is tied to your growth in spiritual awareness. There are essentials to apply daily for this spiritual growth as recorded in the Book of Acts. There are five areas to master. We must: read our word, pray, witness, be relational and obey God. Tremendous growth can happen if we make collective efforts to engage in these five fundamental areas. The first two deal with our vertical relationship with God, which is critical to our enduring sustainability. The last three deal with our horizontal relationship with God in showing our love to Him. Jesus said: "If you love me, keep my commandments." [John 14:15] We show this when we express God to others. We accepted Christ by faith. We must now do better at living in our faith so we can see more clearly His power released in the earthly realm through our actions. It's valuable to spend time reflecting on where you need to be more targeted in these areas for spiritual growth. "Whoever sows to the spirit will reap from the spirit, eternal life." [Galatians 6:8]

Spend at least 15 minutes each day in quiet introspection.
Turn off the TV. Walk around the block or in your yard. Breathe
in nature's purifying air to clear away heady thoughts.
And tune into your heart's soulful silence to become more aware
of His word.

My thoughts:

_____
_____
_____
_____

JUNE
DAY 10

It's common to change our points of view when a situation impacts our life in emotionally. Those who lack resources may react as though the world owed them something, while those who have abundance may have the opinion that they owe the world and want to give back to show their gratitude. Taking these two examples to another level, what if the man who had previously lacked wins the lottery, while the man who once had abundance went bankrupt, their view points about life would undoubtedly change. But how do we accept these situations divinely? Consider that whatever we have, it all belongs to God. Whether we have little or a lot, it is enough. "I know how to get along with humble means, and I also know how to live in prosperity; in any and every circumstance I have learned the secret of being filled and going hungry, both of having abundance and suffering need. I can do all things through Him who strengthens me." [Philippians 4:12-13]

Become a conscious Kingdom citizen by acknowledging we're all stewards of the Lord's gifts. We're here on earth to manifest His goodness and bounty, and blessed with a rainbow of experiences to learn that whatever we're blessed with, it's enough to satisfy us divinely.

My thoughts:

_____
_____
_____
_____

JUNE
DAY 11

Pentecost happened fifty days after the crucifixion of our Savior Jesus Christ. This was a sudden move of God impacting those who had gathered for thanksgiving during the "Feast of Weeks." The Book of Acts, second chapter, records: "They were all with one accord in one place." Meaning, they had but one mind and one heart by coming into agreement for a supernatural move of God. Was it the beginning of the last days in the period we live now? The minor Prophet Joel spoke of how on this day God would, "Pour out His spirit on all flesh." [Joel 2:28-32] God's intent, according to the Book of Acts, was to endow the believer for intensified service. Each of you who are filled with the Holy Spirit have been endowed to do supernatural things in God's earthly realm. When Jesus said: "Greater works shall you do," He was speaking of the times we live in now. There has never been a time when we need even more people doing God's work than now. The concerns are with: abortion, poverty, education, the economy and more. All are issues that need the attention of each of you who are called and anointed for service to serve for justice and righteousness! As believers, we must not be afraid to address what we know can keep the people of God from living a blessed and full life. Stand up, for the Lord has released to us the power to get it done!

Fearlessly stand up to help resolve critical issues of the day— issues that are holding us back in every area of our lives.
We're all divine warriors living out God's Word on the battlefield of life!

My thoughts:

_____

_____

_____

_____

JUNE
DAY 12

The Church requires change to bring about perfection. God cares for us more then we care for our own flesh. The mystery of the Church is similar to the relationship of husband and wife. The Church is the Body of Christ. The Church is also seen as a bride or wife. How it can be both is summed up in the mystery revealed by scripture: "and they shall be one." Jesus loves His Body, the Church, and desires to be one in flesh with it. Paul calls this relationship of Christ with the Church as "a great mystery." Jesus loves the Church as His own Body, which indeed it is. From the Church, the Father will receive glory; and by the Church, show forth His wisdom that incorporates His Body, the Church, into His plan for the restoration of all things. Our pursuits should be to magnify Jesus in our bodies, which are individual members of His Body and hence belong to Him. [Ephesians 1:22; Matthew 16:18; Acts 2:47; Colossians 2:17]

Have you thought about how important it is to stay healthy, to be able to carry out God's mission for you?
God cares more for us more than we do our bodies. We need to keep the physical in as perfect condition as possible, in maintaining healthy, dynamic bodies. Healthiness is next to godliness.
Be sure to schedule those annual medical and dental checkups to stay healthy and happy.

My thoughts:

_____
_____
_____
_____

JUNE
DAY 13

"O taste and see that the Lord is good: blessed is the man that trusteth in him." [Psalm 34:8] It has not been revealed to you all of the wonderful things that God has in store for them that will trust Him.

Our unwavering trust in God reaps the undeniable payoff of being taken care of not only now, but also eternally.
When things are not happening as your mind expects, cast off self-doubt, jealousy and any uncomely expectations—to renew your faith in His work.
Learn the art of patience in trusting God's grace to unfold at His own time.

My thoughts:

_____

_____

_____

_____

JUNE
DAY 14

What do you see when you look in the mirror? Do you see joy unspeakable, health and prosperity? Or is it a vision of helplessness, despair and futility? Is the image that reflects back representative of the person that you believe you are? You must see yourself as God sees you. You are the righteousness of God. "For He made Him who knew no sin to be sin for us, that we might become the righteousness of God in Him." [2 Corinthians 5:21]

With the grace of the Holy Spirit, we're truly endowed with a wealth of blessings: such as happiness, health and prosperity. If you're in despair now, pray for your soul's light to emerge and to shine upon your darkness, in showing you a wealth of possibilities and opportunities to overcome fleeting obstacles.

My thoughts:

_____

_____

_____

_____

JUNE
DAY 15

God loves us unconditionally. When we sin, He forgives us, finds a way to help us learn from the error and continues to love us. He separates us from unrighteous behavior and brings us to a place of enlightenment and healing. As followers of Christ, not only must we forgive others, but also and foremost, forgive ourselves. "Bearing with one another, and forgiving each other, whoever has a complaint against anyone; just as the Lord forgave you, so also should you." [Colossians 3:13] Let your life be a testimony to others of just how good God really is. Only you can tell that story. Don't allow unforgiveness (along with the guilt and condemnation that it breeds) to keep you from freeing someone else through your testimony.

God forgives us all the time; realize this is the name of the divine game.
Then, learn to forgive yourself, and others.

My thoughts:

_____

_____

_____

_____

JUNE
DAY 16

God wants us to fellowship with each other at church. This may seem challenging because it looks like we only know each other superficially. In Acts 2:42, it's clear that with birthing the Church, God meant for us to fellowship one with another. Luke said in this passage: "And they continued steadfastly in the Apostles doctrine, and fellowship, in the breaking of breading, and in prayers." There are four emphases; one of them is fellowship. Fellowship in Greek ("koinonia") means: partnership, unity, close association, society, brotherhood and sharing. God wants Church members to be in partnership with one another to grow spiritually stronger. If we're going to experience vital growth individually and corporately in the church, we must be relational with each other. This allows us to walk in a horizontal relationship with the Lord, in furthering His will. Reach out to those you serve with, to get to know them in the spirit, too. Greater increase will also come into your life because He will use His people to bless you with more.

We reap as we sow. Everyone's heartfelt bonds of spiritual fellowship are priceless in helping us grow spiritually, and to prosper from our networking efforts.
Kingdom citizens are vital for coming together to grow and bring prosperity to our church and ourselves. Who knows what networking among your brothers and sisters will yield?

My thoughts:

_____
_____
_____
_____

JUNE
DAY 17

There is no sibling rivalry with our savior Jesus. The Spirit Himself testifies with our spirit that we are children of God; and if children, heirs also, heirs of God and fellow heirs with Christ. If indeed we suffer with Him, so we may also be glorified with Him. [Romans 8:16-17] We have inherited a great treasure. This is the gift that God has given us—a wonderful elder brother, Jesus, who makes the path of salvation bright because He is on the way. This is a new birth, as we're chosen by God to sit at the head and fellowship with God and man. We are now born into the family of God. Therefore if any man be in Christ, he is a new creature: old things are passed away; behold, all things are become new. [2 Corinthians 5:17]

We're all children of God—and He so loves us that He sent Jesus Christ to teach us to unlearn the folly of our old, unfruitful ways. Why? That's because God wants us to learn anew our fellowship in Him and with all of mankind.

My thoughts:

_____

_____

_____

_____

JUNE
DAY 18

"When I was a child, I spake as a child, I understood as a child, I thought as a child: but when I became a man, I put away childish things." [1 Corinthians 13:11] But as we mature into adulthood and assume more responsibilities of parenthood and citizenship, let us also not forget the divine childlike consciousness in us. We are our Father's children, regardless of whether we're twenty, fifty or ninety years old. Hang on to that sense of humor and fun. God does want us to stay happy, unfettered by worries and fears—and rightfully so, as children of God.

There's a world of difference between being childish and childlike.
Children are innocent and pure in their approach to all, including adults.
Use your pure heart to identify with others while manifesting God's Glory.

My thoughts:

_____

_____

_____

_____

JUNE
DAY 19

Change for adults doesn't come cheap or easy. It costs a death to the old, to experience a birth of the new. We havn't put the child in us to death yet. As Abraham offered up his young son, so must we offer up our immaturity. Why? Like Abraham, we must do it because God requires it. We must bring our childish immaturity to the altar for transformation if we're to pass over to the other side of a real experience with God. We must realize no one can do it for us, but ourselves. You alone can make this personal offering to God. Unfortunately, many of us are stuck in the middle of the lake because a storm arose and we failed to offer up our childish issues when we were supposed to. We could not, or would not, give up our immature ways, thoughts or actions; so now we're rocking in the boat of mediocrity. Instead, we could have crossed over into abundance (which represents wholeness, contentment and tranquility) which are rightfully ours.

God wants us to fulfill Him—from experiencing His wealth of joy, contentment, peace and harmony He graciously gifts everyone.
We can rightfully tap into His treasures by giving up childish expectations of the earthly realm.

My thoughts:

_____

_____

_____

_____

JUNE
DAY 20

It's amazing how Christians think we've given up so much, to obey and serve our Father. But nothing could be further from the truth! Nothing is lost when you serve Jesus. The Lord Jesus Christ promised: "Every one that hath forsaken houses, or brethren, or sisters, or father, or mother, or wife, or children, or lands, for My Name's sake, shall receive an hundredfold, and shall inherit everlasting life." [Matthew 19:29] God will command His blessings upon you—but only when your commitment to Him is steadfast and true. God said if you serve Him, He'll bless your bread and your water; and take sickness away from the midst of you. [Exodus 23:25] As you abide in Christ, God will multiply, keep, protect and watch over you. He will drive the enemy away from you. Remember Job when he thought he had lost everything, yet recovered it all? Even at his lowest point Job prayed: "I know that Thou canst do every thing, and that no thought can be withholden from Thee." [Job 42:2] Job's trust in the Lord remained strong and true despite his misfortunes. The Lord was pleased with Job and gave him double for his trouble! No loss, only gain.

Never feel God has forsaken you—especially when facing roadblocks.
God is having an experience in and through you as you carry out His Word and work.
Stick with dedicated service to Him, and He'll reward you in His Own Time.

My thoughts:

_____
_____
_____
_____

JUNE
DAY 21

When people witness your weakness, it gives them so much power over you. But the issue is not about who's having power. The question is: What would you do with that power? Jesus brought it home and made it real when one morning, the scribes and Pharisees brought a woman to him, who had been caught in adultery. After much questioning of Him, he told the snarling religious mob, "Let he who is without sin cast the first stone." [John 8:7] One by one the crowd dispersed until none of her accusers were present. She was clearly guilty and scripturally inexcusable; yet Jesus told her that since no one else was there to accuse her, He wouldn't accuse her either. He told her to sin no more, and not expect herself to be perfect from then on. But rather, to be always mindful of the grace she had received. In other words, we should learn from our mistakes—not continue in the same vein of sin.

No one is ever "perfect," except God.
Yes, practice makes perfect—but only up to one particular point.
In the process of seeking ongoing perfection, we must know it's a
never-ending spiral where attaining one goal is but the starting
point for another, more elevating goal.

My thoughts:

_____

_____

_____

_____

JUNE
DAY 22

Maintaining our horizontal relationship with God is essential to our soul's salvation. "Let us hold fast the confession of our hope without wavering, for He who promised is faithful." [Hebrews 10:23] Many of us quit too easily. When things go wrong or they don't fall in place as we'd hoped, we stop coming to church. We stop worshiping God, stop participating in choir—when we should be running harder and faster to church to get our spiritual tune-up. Additionlly, "Not forsaking the assembling of ourselves together as is the manner of some, but exhorting one another, and so much more as you see the day approaching." God means for us to be able to get what we need in His house and as well, for us to impact those in attendance. God wants to use us in His house to manifest Himself in and through us. But you have to be in fellowship with others for Him to do that. Stay connected in service and worship the Lord beyond measure.

Unity in oneness among Kingdom citizens uplifts our collective efforts in serving the Lord.
United we stand, divided we fall.
Stand tall in forsaking all that's bothering you; instead, place your trust in manifesting Him, along with your brothers and sisters.

My thoughts:

_____

_____

_____

_____

JUNE
DAY 23

Meditate on the word of God day and night. "But his delight is in the law of the Lord; and in his law doth he meditate day and night. And he shall be like a tree planted by the rivers of water, that bringeth forth his fruit in his season; his leaf also shall not wither; and whatsoever he doeth shall prosper. [Psalm 1:2-3] There are many benefits to meditating: improving concentration, general health, athletic performance, decreasing respiratory rates, relaxing naturally, lowering blood pressure levels and building self-confidence. When you add the Word of God to your meditation regimen it will prove powerful and practical!

Meditation is both a spiritual and a practical lifestyle tool.
Meditation is a natural and practical life activity—just like drinking water.
What's more natural than drinking the Father's life-giving and thirst-quenching Word?

My thoughts:

_____

_____

_____

_____

JUNE
DAY 24

The world can be confused about who Christians are. These misconceptions are also fed by our inability to step out in our true colors, to show up for what we really believe in. Your workplace doesn't need a sermon; they could get that on television. Your job, however, is your practical pulpit to show your true Christian colors. How you conduct yourself should reflect what you believe in and serve as a testimony to God's Will. Some may protest it's difficult to maintain Christian integrity when you have to deal with negativity, corporate sabotage, unethical management and the misuse of power. How can you stand firm when the enemy is all around, trying to pull you down? Actually, Christians can be at their best when the enemy comes. The anointing is activated by the enemy encroachment. As situations get worse, God will increase the anointing. Sometimes we have to get more creative as challenges enlarge or intensify. You may have to step outside the situation to remind yourself as to who put you there, first. Leave your office, take a break, and call on God for help. God is very present in times of trouble. Learn to call on Him instead of falling into the enemy's trap, to avoid them winning wars! When adversity and challenges attack, remember this: I can do all things through Christ, Who strengthens me! [Philippians 4:13]

"The enemy" is all around us. That's why life is such a battlefield.
But our steadfastness in prevailing upon our Heavenly Father is the greatest strength we can cultivate to be always victorious.

My thoughts:

_____

_____

_____

_____

181

JUNE
DAY 25

Have you heard any good news lately? Seems like news these days center mainly around negative stories or some injustice done to a group or race of people. The good news that we have to share is: the true and risen Saviour. The headline doesn't change that He lives. You also were included in Christ when you heard the message of truth, the gospel of your salvation—and believed in it. When you believed, you were marked in Him with a seal, the promised Holy Spirit. [Ephesians 1:13]

Pass along and share the word that when we believe in Christ, we're positive newsmakers.
The good news is we're eternal—thanks to God's goodness saving us, time and again.

My thoughts:

_____
_____
_____
_____

JUNE
DAY 26

Pentecost is a sign that Jesus is Lord. As believers, we have the privilege of showing the world that Jesus is Lord of our lives by living a Holy Spirit-led life. Paul said, "I urge you to walk worthy of the calling with which you were called." [Ephesians 4:1] Walking worthy means being connected to the church where God has called you. Hebrews says: "Forsake not the assembly of yourselves." Walking worthy means bringing tithes and offerings, even when you're not there. "Will a man rob God, yet you have robbed me." [Malachi 3:8] Walking worthy means to be forgiving at all times. John says: "If you forgive the sins of any they are forgiven." When you live a Spirit-led life, according to Paul, you can be called a son of God: "For as many as are led by the Spirit of God these are sons of God." [Romans 8:14] Are you living a Spirit-led life?

List three ways for a Spirit-led life; how will you implement them in your daily activities?
When you give unconditionally of your resources to the house of God, He welcomes not robbing others of their need when they turn to the church for help.
God will bless you with over-abundance; give and it will be given back to you manifold.

My thoughts:

_____

_____

_____

_____

JUNE
DAY 27

Also I heard the voice of the Lord, saying, "Whom shall I send, and who will go for us? Then said I, Here am I; send me." [Isaiah 6:8] Listen intently for the voice of the Lord. He needs a willing vessel. Pray and spend quiet time meditating daily on God's plan for you.

When you hear God's voice, be ever ready to love and serve Him in those who need your help.
Whatever you do for God with a pure heart and good intentions will return in over-abundance to you.

My thoughts:

_____
_____
_____
_____

JUNE
DAY 28

Many struggle, in wondering if they've been completely forgiven by God of their past sins. That stems from how the world deals with us when they know even only a little of our past transgressions. People say they've forgiven and moved on, but because of their subsequent actions, that seems far from the truth in most cases. God says: "I, even I, am He who blots out your transgressions for My sake: and I will not remember your sins." [Isaiah 43:25] We can be confident in knowing that God wipes our slate clean to never ever remember our iniquities—which is why He gave us His only begotten Son. Jesus Christ died to pay the debts of our sins so we might be free. Interestingly, Jesus said: "But if we walk in the light as He is in the Light, we have fellowship with one another, and the blood of Jesus Christ His Son cleanses us from all sin." [1 John 1:7]

Are we living in a culture of negativity? Advertisers say it takes 10 repetitions to get a favorable hit, but only 3 for a negative view.
As a Kingdom citizen, raise the bar and walk in His Word, with positive encouragement for everyone to bring out their best!

My thoughts:
_____
_____
_____
_____

JUNE
DAY 29

When we become followers of Christ, we put on the new man, or woman. We put off old behaviors, attitudes and signs that have held us back for so long, from having belonged to Satan's dark forces of self-destruction. God has brought us out of darkness into the light to realize and fulfill Him with the unlimited potential He's blessed us with. "Wherefore he saith, Awake thou that sleepest, and arise from the dead, and Christ shall give thee light." [Ephesians 5:14]

Aim higher to realize your unlimited potential that God has blessed you and everyone with.
Consciously manifest ongoing change—in disavowing those old forces of self-destruction and self-inflicted darkness—to truly realize your highest, most awesome divine potential!

My thoughts:

_____
_____
_____
_____

JUNE
DAY 30

Education is a key to growth in our communities, region and country. The importance of education is being expressed in all sorts of venues and media outlets. Teachers, parents and principals encourage men, women and children to arm themselves with education. Education increases knowledge. Knowledge is power. Therefore, learn all you can to enhance your self-esteem, increase your knowledge and wisdom—to better stay on an even playing field with others in your circle of influence. "Study to shew thyself approved unto God, a workman that needeth not to be ashamed, rightly dividing the word of truth." [2 Timothy 2:15]

Educate yourself with the power of wisdom that translates into powerful results of self-esteem, prosperity and meaningful living. Understanding God's Word is the secret key to leveling the playing field with others in every area of your personal and professional life!

My thoughts:

_____

_____

_____

_____

JULY
DAY 1

Every day, we must pursue God's agenda for our lives to remain in His perfect will. Paul advacates: "I press toward the goal for the prize of the upward call of God in Christ Jesus." [Phillipians 3:14] Often, we allow our baggage and unfounded fears to hold us back, to put off doing what was meant for today, until tomorrow. To be all that we can be, we must keep Christ as our primary pursuit; meaning, we must keep first things first. This is the ultimate! But unfortunately, we give too much attention to "loud" things in our lives which seem to be more urgent. Or put off facing hard, unpleasant, things. Paul's focus was on the ultimate four things he knew he had to work on to get back on track: 1) Yourself. You are your greatest asset or worst liability. 2) Your priorities. You must fight for the important ones. 3) Work on your strengthens. You can reach your boundless potential! 4) Work with others. You can't be effective working alone. Keep Christ as Your Primary Pursuit to enrich your life.

Reflect on your core strengths to reinforce all the more, to better pursue God's agenda.
Write them down and meditate on how you'll use them wisely in practical situations to share God's power with others—shopping (as a gracious shopper) or courteous driver (not getting mad behind the wheel).
How will you strengthen your powers and offer them selflessly, in practical ways?

My thoughts:

_____

_____

_____

_____

JULY
DAY 2

The Lord loves it when we communicate with him in prayer. Therefore, never be afraid to call on Him as often as you feel you need to. As the Bible reminds us, He lets us know that He will always answer the call of those who keep His ways. "I call on you, my God, for you will answer me; turn your ear to me and hear my prayer." [Psalm 17:6] He has a remedy for whatever ails us and is waiting to give us His absolute best. When we call on Him, He gives us the assurance of victory. "As for me, I will call upon God, and the Lord shall save me. Evening and morning and at noon I will pray and cry aloud. And He shall hear my voice." [Psalm 55:16-17]

God is everywhere and hears our cries for help, anytime we remember to pray with intensity and sincerity.
However, learn the art of patience and gratefully await God's answers and guidance.

My thoughts:

_____

_____

_____

_____

JULY
DAY 3

Saint Augustine's strategy for building asks: Do you wish to rise? Begin by descending. You plan a tower that will pierce the clouds? Lay first the foundation of humility. Your sure foundation must be sturdy enough to secure the greatness that you shall achieve on your Christian journey. It's invigorating to build based on the blueprint that the Father has designed because we know the outcome will be awesome—to have a more abundant life. He has devised the plan for our life journey, brick by brick. To put others first is the first brick to the foundation leading to humility. Jesus was our example; He lived to give His life as ransom for mankind. He was the greatest among men, yet was servant to all. Having a mind to serve is the greatest display of humility. The depths of your servitude will determine the heights that you will soar to. "But he who is greatest among you shall be your servant. And whoever exalts himself will be humbled, and he who humbles himself will be exalted." [Matthew 23:11-12]

Humility is the ability to selflessly serve others and to bring them joy.
What are some humble acts of service you're most proud of?
How else can you extend your life of humility and selfless service to live in His word?

My thoughts:

_____

_____

_____

_____

JULY
DAY 4

As children in our parents' homes, we were anxious to grow up, experience freedom away from our parents' rule and do whatever we wanted to. We were in a hurry to make our own decisions, to come and go as we pleased. But what we didn't realize then was, this kind of freedom came with a price. Once adults, we quickly learned that adulthood in all of its benefits carried many responsibilities. Although we can't return to our childhood as adults, many of us wish we could have savored the time spent being children. As children of God, we receive liberty in Christ Jesus. Christ has made us free. We're brought into a state of divine grace and liberty—no longer in bondage to our old sinful ways. Neither are we tied to the curse of the law. We owe this liberty to Jesus Christ who once and for all freed us when He died at Calvary. On the contrary, we should have no desire to return to what Christ saved us from. We're now free to live, free to love and free to understand and obey the principles that gift us the abundant life Christ promises—if we but obey God's Commandments. "Stand fast therefore in the liberty by which Christ has made us free, and do not be entangled again with a yoke of bondage." [Galatians 5:1]

The real freedom is to live in the way of the Lord—not what our egos and minds willfully demand.
Obedience in doing His Will is the highest form of freedom.

My thoughts:

_____

_____

_____

_____

JULY
DAY 5

God is a true gentleman. "For God is not unjust to forget your work and labor of love which you have shown toward His name, in that you have ministered to the saints, and do minister." [Hebrews 6:10] No matter what you're doing in the Kingdom (ushering, youth ministry, song ministry, prayer team, preaching, follow up, evangelism) we do it in the name of Jesus. It's important for us to recognize there'll always be those whom we've ministered to and those who are to come. We must be ready and prepared, regardless of what's going on in our lives. In this season of summer, when our energies are even more dynamic and powerful, we must overcome sluggishness. This is the time to really step it up with the abundant opportunities before us. There are more people out and about in our neighborhoods, city and everywhere else, than there are during the winter months. This is the time to evangelize and minister unto those who need a fresh word from the Lord. "That you do not become sluggish (lazy) but imitate those who through faith and patience inherit the promises." [Hebrews 6:12]

Summer brings fruitful abundance, in being rich and ripe with the season's offerings.
Count your blessings and share them with righteous word and good deeds!

My thoughts:

_____
_____
_____
_____

JULY
DAY 6

Circumstances of life shape us and make us who God has designed us to be. To be spiritually renewed is something that every Christian should strive to achieve. How beautiful is the butterfly. It displays many different colors, in reflecting the journey it has taken. It can represent the carefree transformative nature in us as new creatures in Christ. We're all unique in many ways, yet are similar, too. We go through similar situations in life, but these have different effects on us and can cause different outcomes. Each of these situations and experiences make us who we are and shape us into who we are to become. Celebrate your newness as you transform from the old to the new. Life becomes a collage and our story a kaleidoscope. When we combine all of the colors of our life, it makes our world beautiful. "Therefore if any man be in Christ, he is a new creature: old things are passed away; behold all things are become new." [2 Corinthians 5:17]

God is constantly creating newness in His creation—with people, the environment and amazing revelations.
Learn to shed old thoughts and outdated ideas, and learn to master the art of going with the flow of adapting to and trying out innovations.
If they don't work out, don't give up; just try different new ways of achieving your goals. Success comes with persistence and the courage to be continuously renewed spiritually.

My thoughts:

_____
_____
_____
_____

JULY
DAY 7

As believers, we must work to put on the "new man." Paul urged us to: "Be renewed in the spirit of your mind." [Ephesians. 4:23] The mind can cause us to walk contrary to the ways of God. Which then causes our conduct to grow corrupt. Paul admonished: "You should no longer walk as the Gentiles walk, in the futility of their mind." Futility means emptiness or purposelessness caused by this state of mind in becoming directionless with no goals in life for living better. We musn't ever become alienated from God, or cease to care about ourselves, others and life in general. God has better for us when we walk in righteousness and holiness. We must have a desire to grow and pursue our God-blessed power with positively divine abandonment. Giving ourselves over to God for His good use is the right thing to do, to absolutely bring Him glory.

Be constantly renewed by your spiritual mind that's nourished by the light of your soul.
This is the simple secret for staying on track and being constantly renewed—by meditating on God's Will with our soul's aspiration, and singing His Glory.

My thoughts:

_____

_____

_____

_____

JULY
DAY 8

No one goes through life without facing temptation. Temptations are tests of opportunities to sin against God. "Blessed is the man that endureth temptation: for when he is tried, he shall receive the crown of life, which the Lord hath promised to them that love him." [James 1:12] Some temptations are bigger while some may seem small. When a great temptation arises, those who work to overcome will attempt to alleviate the source of that temptation. Where the temptation is small, we must pay just as much attention, lest giving in to these small temptations become a habit and before long become a necessity (such as alcohol). Overcoming temptations strengthens our faith. James shows how we can profit from our trials. "My brethren, count it all joy when you fall into various trials, knowing that the testing of your faith produces patience. But let patience have its perfect work, that you may be perfect and complete, lacking nothing." [James 1:2-4]

When temptation strikes, pray hard, intensely, plus sincerely—
for God's grace to help you bravely face it and to overcome it;
it's very important to first acknowledge the problem exists.
Second, your courage to be saved will move God to grant you the
divine weapons needed to vanquish the problem.

My thoughts:

_____

_____

_____

_____

JULY
DAY 9

Spiritual growth doesn't "just happen," anymore than climbing a mountain happens without hard training and perseverance. You don't wander up a mountain and surprise yourself when you reach the top. Growth results from hard work. Paul said: "As you therefore have received Christ Jesus the Lord, so walk in Him, rooted and built up in Him and established in the faith, as you have been taught, abounding in it with thanksgiving." [Colossians 2:6-7] When you take seed, soil, sunshine and water, then mix them up, you don't get a plant overnight. You need time. Paul knew the Colossians' roots wouldn't grow deep overnight. So he reminded them of eight attributes that must happen for growth to occur: labor, stretching, learning, focus, accountability, building on the past, consistent application and gratitude. Consider this process as you grow in the Lord.

Gratitude is the divine key of spiritual growth to enter God's Heart-Palace.
Offering thanks to walk in His grace as we go about our Father's business is a practical spiritual application while acknowledging His Presence in our lives.
Giving thanks also silently invokes His constant blessings, guidance and protection.

My thoughts:
_____
_____
_____
_____

JULY
DAY 10

1 Corinthians 14:1 takes a look at the gifts of tongues and prophecy. Paul had written a letter to the church at Corinth to realign them more properly into God's business because they had began to pervert the gifts of the Holy Spirit. As believers we must, and should, operate in an orderly way when flowing in our God-blessed gifts. Paul told the church they should: "desire the best gifts." Yes, you're filled with the Holy Spirit. And we know the gift of tongues is released to us as we receive the Spirit. But, what have you desired since being filled with the Holy Spirit? We should all be longing for God to release more of His gifts so we would experience God in different, more fulfilling ways. This enriches us and everyone else even more, as we come together to worship Him. It's opportune to seek God for more of His gifts to enable us to operate at higher levels, as God's representatives. And as well, enrich and endow greater blessings unto our regions.

Open your heart sincerely to better receive the Holy Spirit—by meditating on God's Will.
What are some flashes of divine inspiration flowing through your consciousness?
Write them down; regularly refer to them as you aspire to selflessly offer only the best gifts.

My thoughts:

_____

_____

_____

_____

JULY
DAY 11

Scientific studies show eagles soar as high as 10,000 feet or 3,048 meters. Are you ready to soar to amazing heights? Eagles in the Bible represent: protectors, carriers of prayers; and beings that bring strength, courage and wisdom. "You yourselves have seen what I did to the Egyptians, and how I bore you on eagles' wings and brought you to myself." [Exodus 19:4] Eagles also symbolize healing and creation, while possessing great beauty, tremendous strength and skill. How high will you fly with the right wind beneath your wings? The strength of the Lord is your wind. "But they that wait upon the Lord shall renew their strength; they shall mount up with wings as eagles; they shall run, and not be weary; and they shall walk, and not faint." [Isaiah 40:31]

Strive to fly as high as you can with your God-blessed skills, talents and strengths.
Live each day as best you can to realize these gifts, in serving God more meaningfully.

My thoughts:

_____

_____

_____

_____

JULY
DAY 12

"Greater is He that is in you, than he that is in the world." [1 John 4:4] John said we're people who overcome adversity based on Who is living in us. "Greater is He" means the power of God residing in us. So that the enemy chasing us, bothering us, speaking evil of us, or trying to make us fall hard is less than the power that God has placed in us. You can overcome everything the enemy tries to put in your path! But you have to be willing, ready and eager to be led by the Holy Spirit.

We're protected by the divine sanctity of our homes. When leaving this sanctuary of hearth and home, offer a minute of silence to consciously invoke God's protection before heading out.
And thus have the confidence of walking in His Way, all day. What other practical ways can you invoke, and be led by, the Holy Spirit in daily living?

My thoughts:

_____
_____
_____
_____

JULY
DAY 13

Have you ever felt lost? Not in the sense of having no directions in arriving at destinations, but lost in the love of the Lord? "I have been crucified with Christ; it is no longer I who live, but Christ lives in me; and the life which I now live in the flesh I live by faith in the Son of God, who loved me and gave Himself for me." [Galatians 2:20]

God created everyone with a specific purpose to manifest Him.
This is a deeper question to figure out—of what your life's purpose is all about.
Pray and meditate on His grace to help you gradually figure out your life's mission, while living in His love more purposefully.

My thoughts:

_____
_____
_____
_____

JULY
DAY 14

Various types of insurance can be purchased to protect against loss of life, health, home and auto; even the loss of a pet. To help mitigate the risk of financial devastation in the event of losses, we consider it a moral responsibility to acquire relevant kinds of insurance. To be a follower of Christ though, is to be eternally insured. The Lord is our protection against the chance of loss. We never have to be found without God's protection. God's protection is insurance for the believer. It provides the assurance we need to give us peace of mind. God promises the kind of peace that surpasses all understanding. When you put your trust and faith in God, you're in the best of hands. "For in the time of trouble, He shall hide me in His pavilion; In the secret place of His tabernacle He shall hide me, he shall set me high upon a rock." [Psalm 27:5]

Faith in God is the ultimate insurance—this lifetime and eternally.
Since we're of God and always for Him, we're divinely insured as His children
Will any father ever fail their child? No; more so in God's case.

My thoughts:

_____

_____

_____

_____

JULY
DAY 15

You are a candidate for leadership in the kingdom of God. You can be trusted to study the Word of God and deliver it with the preciseness that the Lord reveals to you. You have the potential to be a great leader. As you're developing this gift of leadership, pray for God to grant you spiritual insight as it applies to the scriptures. He will help you remain pure and protect you from the work of Satan. [Psalm 121:7] The scriptures promise you'll grow and be strengthened as you walk with the Lord. Grow in the grace and knowledge of our Lord and Savior Jesus Christ. "To Him be the glory, both now and to the day of eternity. Amen." [2 Peter 3:18]

Your potential to grow into a trusted leader in God's army is a given.
Pray to God for spiritual insight to more properly develop this gift for His mission.

My thoughts:

_____

_____

_____

_____

JULY
DAY 16

To grow in Christ, we must reflect Christ's attributes to the world as Christ displayed them while He walked on earth. We show dedicated servitude through the love that we show to others. We have to desire to be like Christ—but we have to desire to know him first. We have to know His ways, what pleases Him and what displeases Him. We know that without faith, it's impossible to please Him. [Hebrews 11:6] Therefore, have faith. Then, we have to obey without question what the Lord has asked us to do. He says to love, which is the first and greatest commandment. [Mark 12:30] We should love how He loves us. How to? He served. "Yet it shall not be so among you; but whoever desires to become great among you shall be your servant. And whoever of you desires to be first shall be slave of all. For even the Son of Man did not come to be served, but to serve, and to give His life a ransom for many." [Mark 10:42-45]

Christ served, and continues to serve, with unconditional love. That's how we continue to serve our brethren with love, joy and a peaceful heart.

My thoughts:

_____

_____

_____

_____

JULY
DAY 17

"God always was and always will be." [John 1:1] In the beginning was the Word, and the Word was with God, and the Word was God. But we must be in Him; we must know Him intimately and divinely. "The Holy Spirit is not a human touch or an external breath. He is the Almighty God. He is a Godly Presence in every person, residing in the depths of our souls. He is the Holy One dwelling in the temple not made with hands." [2 Corinthians 5:1] "Beloved, He touches, and it is done. He is the same God over all, who is rich unto all who call upon Him." [Romans 10:12]

The body is the temple wherein Almighty God the Holy Spirit resides, in the depths of our souls.
Our souls offer constant, boundless nourishment and guidance. Meditate daily to tap into the Holy Spirit to better hear the voice of conscience to engage in sound decision-making and be intuitively guided in all things.
It's important to keep the physical body functioning properly to do God's work. So don't forget to eat healthily, exercise and schedule those annual checkups.

My thoughts:
_____
_____
_____
_____

JULY
DAY 18

The power of the Holy Spirit is clear to all who believe in the Lord Jesus Christ. "But if the Spirit of Him who raised Jesus from the dead dwells in you, He who raised Christ Jesus from the dead will also give life to your mortal bodies through His Spirit who dwells in you." [Romans 8:11] This power gives supernatural wisdom to provide godly counsel to those in need. We should always look to God to constantly fill us with the overflowing presence and power of the Holy Spirit. The power of the Holy Spirit fills us with joy and in giving us a profound understanding of every principle of the Bible. Thank God for this power that comes from God alone. "Now may the God of hope fill you with all joy and peace in believing, that you may abound in hope by the power of the Holy Spirit." [Romans 15:13]

The Holy Spirit resides in everyone.
We only have to become conscious of this fact of life.
Through daily prayer and meditation, we get to know the Holy Spirit intimately—to help us make progress with our life's journey.

My thoughts:

_____

_____

_____

_____

JULY
DAY 19

There is nothing outside God's salvation. Nothing! We're filled, immersed and clothed only by the grace of the Holy Spirit. There is nothing felt, seen or spoken about—except in the mighty power of the Holy Spirit. We're new creatures in Christ Jesus, baptized into a new nature. "He who believes in Me, as the Scripture has said, out of his heart will flow rivers of living water." [John 7:38] The very life of the Risen Christ is to be in everything we are and do, in moving us to do His Will.

When we're into the Holy Spirit, everything flows smoothly for us and those around.
Seemingly unfriendly folks will melt when they feel our wordless care and concern for them.
Seemingly unworkable workplace projects will resonate with amicable oneness when we prevail upon Him to occupy His business towards the goal of fruitful team productivity.

My thoughts:

_____

_____

_____

_____

JULY
DAY 20

There are those who will try to lead you from the path that God has designed for you to walk on. Don't be surprised by people who have broken ranks from the righteous path. The Bible warns these are people who don't have the Spirit of God and who have followed their lower human instincts. It's important you stay focused. Your gifts are needed at this hour. It's important to pray to build up your faith to not be led astray. Jesus, in speaking to Peter, told him Satan was trying to separate him from the brethren and also from Jesus. "Simon, Simon, behold, Satan has demanded permission to sift you like wheat; but I have prayed for you, that your faith may not fail; and you, when once you have turned again, strengthen your brothers." [Luke 22:31-32] Unless we watch and pray, we're all subject to temptations that could draw us back into sin. This is why prayer is important. "But ye beloved, building up yourselves on your most holy faith, praying in the Holy Ghost." [Jude 1:20]

Our sincere and intense prayers are divine armor and weapons of protection from dark forces.
We have to be ever vigilant in not letting down our divine armor, especially in the face of temptation.

My thoughts:

_____
_____
_____
_____

JULY
DAY 21

What does it take to grow an effective ministry? Confidence and expectation are critical for an effective ministry. A successful ministry is the product of: our faith; the assignment that God has given us; combined with the spiritual foundation that we build. We need a powerful ministry that is long-lasting and life-changing. This type of progressive ministry is built on solid foundational principals established in the Word of God. To the degree that you have cultivated a conviction in these principals, you will not waver in the days to come. [Psalm 55:22]

Fully participate in growing your church ministry teams to reflect your collective assignments from God.
There are many dynamic projects to throw your heart and soul into, to manifest God's word.
Look around and see which Kingdom activities interest you; then ask an Elder or other leader for guidance.

My thoughts:

_____

_____

_____

_____

JULY
DAY 22

You are blessed with a perpetual blessing. You have to decide that you're going with the proven order of God. When you do this in consecration, God will establish you and your heritage forever. This is always to be the perpetual share from the Israelites for Aaron and his sons. It is the contribution the Israelites are to make to the Lord from their fellowship offerings. [Exodus 29:28]

When we fully consecrate our lives to God, He takes care of us eternally.
Consecrating our lives to Him need not be fearful—but a totally natural acceptance of our life's deeper spiritual mission.

My thoughts:

_____
_____
_____
_____

JULY
DAY 23

The Bible cautions us against being unequally yoked. "Be ye not unequally yoked together with unbelievers: for what fellowship hath righteousness with unrighteousness? and what communion hath light with darkness?" [2 Corinthians 6:14] We don't associate with those who don't share the same values, ideas or moral convictions as we do. Scripture warns us to separate ourselves from such people. Separation generally carries a negative connotation. But in the body of Christ, separation is good. We have to learn the art of divine separation and wise discernment. It's important to separate or detach yourself from anything and anybody that interferes with what God has called you to do. You don't want to leave this earth not having fulfilled your purpose, do you? "Wherefore come out from among them, and be ye separate, saith the Lord, and touch not the unclean thing; and I will receive you." [2 Corinthians 6:17]

Divine detachment is the wisdom of knowing when to disassociate from people, events and things that don't reflect our spiritual values.
Why waste precious time and energy on people who don't believe in walking with the Lord?

My thoughts:

_____

_____

_____

_____

JULY
DAY 24

Take time today to saturate yourself in the word of God. We must make a greater effort to be willing to be drenched in greater knowledge of Him. Devote more time to studying the word of God. Take the time to meditate on the word of God. Make the time to be consumed with the work of God. Ultimately, we must take more than a passive approach to getting more deeply involved in the word of God. "For the word of God is quick, powerful and sharper than any two-edged sword, piercing even to the dividing asunder of soul and spirit, and of the joints and marrow, and is a discerner of the thoughts and intents of the heart. [Hebrews 4:12]

Fully understanding God's word is important to carry out His mission successfully.
Immersing and saturating our consciousness in Him quickens and sharpens us into more powerful instruments.

My thoughts:

_____

_____

_____

_____

JULY
DAY 25

The word of God is the standard for my life. After I have saturated my thinking with the Word of God, it changes how I make decisions. Because now the word of God becomes the standard by which I make all decisions. I weigh everything against God's word. My mind and my thinking have been renewed. "I will make my way prosperous and have good success." [Joshua 1:8]

When we fully uphold God's word in every thought, word and deed, we apply the highest standards to every decision we make. This is also how we make progress with our lives to successfully manifest Him.

My thoughts:

_____

_____

_____

_____

JULY
DAY 26

What are you willing to give up to know Christ better? Are you willing to sacrifice your time for prayer, the approval of your friends, your personal plans or pleasures? Whatever it is, it's worth the sacrifice: "That I may know Him and the power of His Resurrections, and the fellowship of his sufferings, being conformed to His death." [Philippians 3:10]

As Christ gave up His earthly life to free us, we must also sacrifice as needed to become better instruments.
Actually, it isn't sacrifice at all—because we gain so much more in being His conscious instruments to carry out His word.

My thoughts:

_____
_____
_____
_____

JULY
DAY 27

What do you need form the Lord? Jesus said: "So I say to you, ask, and it will be given to you; seek, and you will find; knock, and it will be opened to you. For everyone who asks, receives; and he who seeks, finds; and to him who knocks, it will be opened. [Luke 11:9-10] We cannot think God already knows our needs; therefore, we don't have to ask. It's true God does know what we need before we ask, according to Matthew 6:8: "So do not be like them; for your Father knows what you need before you ask Him." The Bible provides instructions on how to ask so our petitions will be answered. Only God can turn situations around. We understand that nothing is too hard for Him. He can heal cancer, fix a broken marriage, mellow out obstinate children, make a job situation better—even change our financial outlook. The supernatural hand of God always works for you and everyone. You just need to ask, seek and knock on God's heart door.

Although God knows what we need to better fulfill Him, we still need to ask Him first.
Then stay the course and believe you'll be helped and healed according to His will.

My thoughts:

_____

_____

_____

_____

JULY
DAY 28

Stepping into "the gap" is not about shopping for clothes. It's about standing before God and praying on behalf of other people. For thousands of years the first line of defense for a city was the large wall constructed around it. A city could not be taken unless that wall was breached. A gap was a breach or break in the wall that needed to be repaired. Any unrepaired gap allowed the enemy to enter. An intercessor is someone who steps into the gap between God's righteousness and man's failure to recognize His Worth. Through prayer, the intercessor brings the merits of the Cross to bear upon people and situations. Intercessors are needed because the world is filled with people who don't understand the effects of their own sins. Or people don't know or understand God can do everything for them; so they don't know to ask. Many people need someone else to step into their situation in prayer, to step into the gap for them. That's where we come in. We can answer God's call and partner in His Kingdom's purposes by praying for people and situations that need God's healing. "I sought for a man among them who would make a wall, and stand in the gap before Me on behalf of the land, that I should not destroy it; but I found no one." [Ezekiel 22:30] Have you prayed for your family, friends, peers, colleagues, neighborhood, co-workers, church family and those in your region today? Let's stand in the gap in prayer!

When we pray, we must not expect results according to our human and worldly conditions.
The power of prayer uplifts our consciousness when we pray with sincerity, humility, purity and gratitude to be heard by Him. Christ's prayer echoing around the world is: "Thy Will Be Done." End all your prayers thus.

My thoughts:

_____

_____

_____

_____

JULY
DAY 29

For your prayers to be answered, four conditions must be met. 1) We must ask in faith. Whatever you ask, in believing you will receive. [Matthew 21:22] 2) You must be properly motivated. You ask and do not receive because you ask a miss that you may spend it on your pleasures. [James 4:3] 3) You must abide in a relationship with Christ. "If you abide in Me, and My words abide in you, you will ask what you desire and it shall be done for you." [John 15:7] 4) You must ask according to the will of God. This is the confidence which we have before Him, that, if we ask anything according to His will, He hears us. And if we know that He hears us in whatever we ask, we know that we have the requests which we have asked from Him. [1 John 5:14-15]

For our prayers to be answered, we must: ask in faith; be sincerely motivated; have implicit in our relationship with Christ; and ask according to God's will.
Pray soulfully that your prayers are heard according to divine will.

My thoughts:

_____
_____
_____
_____

JULY
DAY 30

We should be very passionate and intense about our relationship with God. God wants every part of you—not just a piece of your mind or a part of your heart. Jesus doesn't ask for a passive commitment to Him. In fact, Jesus asks you to give up everything in order to follow Him, in His grace. We must choose to redirect our focus and passion on the Lord and Him alone. The man at the pool of Bethesda couldn't be healed because he was more concerned with the movement of the water instead of being focused on the One who moved the water. He thought he'd be healed based on what he saw, not based on what he could not see. [John 5:2-3] "Believe on the Lord your God and you shall be saved. And you shall love the Lord your God with all your heart, and with all your soul, and with all your mind, and with all your strength." [Mark 12:30]

We must unequivocally give ourselves over to God with divine passion and intensity.
It's similar to a chef who gives himself or herself over to cooking the most delicious meal.
We should be motivated every day to serve God the most delicious meals with our self-giving.

My thoughts:

_____

_____

_____

_____

JULY
DAY 31

Christians overcome the world by faith. "For whatever is born of God overcomes the world; and this is the victory that has overcome the world—our faith. Who is the one who overcomes the world, but he who believes that Jesus is the Son of God?" [1 John 5:4-5] Are you a believer? In order to enjoy a victory, there must be a struggle or battle of some sort. The battle can be either a natural or spiritual battle. No matter the field, no matter how difficult the fight, we have declared victory over them all. Because we are believers in Jesus Christ, we don't have to be concerned with the fight. The Bible exalts that the battle belongs to the Lord and as such, we have victory because of our faith in Him. [1 Samuel 17:47] There is no greater contender than the Lord God Almighty; and because we're on His side, we *are* assured of victory every time!

God has blessed every fight with victory—of light over darkness. Every fight is based on our implicit faith in God's victory, regardless of external conditions.

My thoughts:
_____
_____
_____
_____

AUGUST
DAY 1

"The righteous shall flourish like a palm tree; He shall grow like a cedar in Lebanon. Those who are planted in the house of the Lord Shall flourish in the courts of our God. They shall still bear fruit in old age; They shall be fresh and flourishing." [Psalm 92:12-14] To flourish is to grow stronger, to develop with vigor and to thrive. The psalmist compares the righteous to palm trees. Fattened trees that flourish represent prosperity and growth. Those who are planted in the house of God provide what is needed to those on the outside. Every branch and fruit is productive and flourishes in the vineyard for years to come. These trees don't just survive but thrive and produce fruitful abundance for the house of God. Unlike a typical tree, the roots of a palm tree don't grow deep, but stand shallow in a ball. To stay strong in withstanding storms, the roots must be stabilized by a force. That force is God. Make sure your godly roots are wrapped up in the heart of God. As you grow and flourish, your branches will reach out into the courtyards where people who need what you have to offer are able to come and bask in your presence, to be nurtured under the branches of your palm tree.

As the saying goes, charity begins at home. Shore up your inner strengths first—from connecting powerfully with God.
As God's power sustains you with His wealth, you'll be able to stand tall and fruitful to share God's gifts with others—and nurture them with your treasures.

My thoughts:

_____
_____
_____
_____

AUGUST
DAY 2

Spiritual growth and the blessings of prosperity begin with wisdom. "Blessed is the man who walks not in the counsel of the ungodly, Nor stands in the path of sinners, Nor sits in the seat of the scornful; But his delight is in the law of the Lord, And in His law he meditates day and night. He shall be like a tree Planted by the rivers of water, That brings forth its fruit in its season, Whose leaf also shall not wither; And whatever he does shall prosper." [Psalm 1:1-3] When a person devotedly does these things according to God's word, he or she prospers. Make no mistake, light and darkness have no communion together; when it comes to your alliance with the ungodly, the psalmist instructs no communion with them, lest we fall into their fate. [2 Corinthians 6:14] He shows the progression to destruction (from walking, standing and sitting with them) to where we get comfortable with the sin and the sinner. On the contrary, the character of a godly man must be maintained by associating yourself with those who are of like mind—while dissociating from those who lead you down the wrong path. Follow this wisdom and you will prosper in His grace!

Sow the seeds of wisdom, and it's inevitable for you to reap God's blessings of prosperity.
Wisdom shows you the way to cultivate godly relationships with people who manifest God's light and fruitful abundance—not with unbelievers bent on leading you astray.

My thoughts:

_____

_____

_____

_____

AUGUST
DAY 3

We are trees of righteousness as Christians, so we must live tall and upright. "That they may be called trees of righteousness, The planting of the lord, that He may be glorified." [Isaiah 61:3] We must not waver in the Lord as we press to mark the highest calling in God. Trees can only bend so much, but they still stand upright in the midst of storms. We are to stand tall and be planted by the rivers of water, so that when troubles come, we faint not. Trees bear fruit, just as Christians faithfully and abundantly bring forth fruit in high season, season after season. As we bear the fruit of spirit, we walk in love, joy, peace, patience, kindness, goodness, faithfulness, meekness, self control; against such, there is no law. [Galatians 5:22-23]

Kingdom citizens must steadfastly offer the fruits of our spiritual growth to manifest God.
It's always fashionable to walk in love and joy, goodness and kindness, peace and serenity,
What else would you like to add?

My thoughts:

_____

_____

_____

_____

AUGUST
DAY 4

Making disciples is our manifestation mandate. The Lord is now enlisting those who will lay aside every encumbrance and entanglements of daily affairs to do all things necessary for the sake of His gospel. One of the most important things is: assist in preparing to do what we do. That is, preparing for minsitry work. When possible, we must do it better than we ever can, to transcend and advance beyond our self-imposed limits whenever possible. Paul said: "He gave some as apostles, and some as prophets, and some as evangelists, and some as pastors, and teachers, for the equipping of the saints for the work of the ministry." [Ephesians 4:11-12]

Spreading the Lord's gospel is not impossible when we overcome our fears and limitations.
Pray for guidance to be relevant to each person you meet, to honestly connect in deeper, more meaningful ways, to show them how they too can live in His Light.

My thoughts:
_____
_____
_____
_____

AUGUST
DAY 5

Many scriptures show how man is tested to see if his faith would endure through a storm or trial. Job was tested and passed with flying colors. [Job 42:10] He even received double for all the trouble he had to endure. God tested Abraham in Genesis 22:1. He tested the children of Israel in Exodus 16:4 to see if they would serve Him through their wilderness experience. As Christians, we're tested daily in one way or another—and presented with a choice to follow God in faith or turn the other way. You may be going through a situation where you feel your faith is being tested. At this hour, you need to know that to remain faithful unto God is the right decision. God is aware of what you're going through and would not allow you to be tempted beyond what you're able to handle. "He will provide a way of escape so that you are able to endure it." [1 Corinthians 10:13] The test you're going through is only to reward you for your obedience to God. "But He knows the way that I take; When He has tested me, I shall come forth as gold. Job 23:10. Continue to love God. Trust and praise Him as you go through the trial. When you have passed the test, you shall receive a crown of life." [James 1:12]

As we're tested at school in order to move on to higher grades, so too is spiritual testing needed to strengthen our determination in making progress with our lives—regardless of our age. The schooling is even better as God is our personal tutor because He blesses us with the needed capacity to handle every test to His satisfaction.

My thoughts:

_____

_____

_____

_____

AUGUST
DAY 6

Jesus said: "You are the world's seasoning, to make it tolerable and to preserve it from corruption." [Matthew 5:13] If you loose your flavor, what will happen to the world? If a seasoning has no flavor, it has no value. If Christians make no effort to have an effect or favorably impact those around them and on the world at large, we're of little value to God. If we're too much like the secular world of non-aspiring people, then we're worthless in carrying out His work. We should affect and impact people positively, just as the careful art of seasoning in knowing what herbs and spices pair well with specific foods brings out the best flavors in feeding your loved ones with healthy, tasty food.

What wholesome, nurturing thoughts would you like to invite today?
What positive qualities make your day more tolerable, such as patience, love and forgiveness—for yourself and others?
And don't forget to smile, whether alone or with others!

My thoughts:

_____
_____
_____
_____

AUGUST
DAY 7

Test the Lord and see that He will keep His word. What a powerful test to be able to give. Because God is, we can be assured He always delivers and won't fail any test. His test is divine and He will not fail. "Bring you all the tithes into the storehouse, that there may be food in my house, and test me now in this, says the Lord of hosts, if I will not open you the windows of heaven, and pour you out a blessing, that there shall not be room enough to receive it." [Malachi 3:8-10] This is a proven test for everyone who obeys the principle of tithing. We're invited to prove what God says by doing a trial run. We cannot lose when we trust God with the tithe—the tenth of our increase. "God is not a man, that He should lie; neither the son of man, that He should repent: hath He said, and shall He not do it? or hath He spoken, and shall He not make it good?" [Numbers 23:19]

God blesses us with gifts galore when we tithe the tenth of our increase.
In giving selflessly, we're blessed with even more—especially from God, the Author of All Good.

My thoughts:

_____

_____

_____

_____

AUGUST
DAY 8

Life is a battelfield, which makes it a trying time for us, all the time. Conditions are always easy for the enemy to step in and wreak havoc to their advantage. Such as causing us to give up on the promises of God. David advised: "Cast our burdens on the Lord and He will sustain us. He shall never suffer the righteous to be moved." [Psalm 55:22] To cast off means to throw away or give up unworthy things that hold us back. We must give up our burdens to the Lord because He can do more for us than we can do for ourselves! We can take long-lasting spiritual comfort in Him because He sustains us eternally through whatever's hurting us. He will not allow our hurts to afflict us forever because we trust Him to resolve them to His satisfaction. Whenever burdens get too heavy to bear, cast them unto the Lord and watch Him bring you out of your depression or unfortunate circumstances. Only be patient and allow Him to work in and through you in His own time.

What is hurting you?
Offer them to the Lord. Bad things are also right to offer to Him so He can transform them to His satisfaction, to help you make spiritual progress.
Again, don't expect results according to human thinking. Just be patient for His divine magic to yield more strength, tolerance or forgiveness—lessons He wants us to learn, in order to unlearn the old.

My thoughts:

_____

_____

_____

_____

AUGUST
DAY 9

Paul was able to look back on his life and testify with conviction that he had done well in maintaining himself as a true soldier while on his Christian journey. He had grown from one who killed Christians to one who would die for the cause of Christ. He is now ready to meet death. For him, this was the end of the road and he felt confident he had carried out the mission, plan and purpose that had been appointed to him by God. "I have fought the good fight, I have finished the race, I have kept the faith." [2 Timothy 4:7] No matter the opposition, he stayed the course. Paul was unwavering in his faith and didn't let anyone or anything deter him from the work of the ministry. He understood the importance of the Lord's work and was committed to the cause of Christ unto death. God sees what you do for Him, and rewards you accordingly. "Therefore, my beloved brothers, be you steadfast, unmovable, always abounding in the work of the Lord, for as much as you know that your labor is not in vain in the Lord." [1 Corinthians 15:58]

How are you maintaining progress on the journey?
What steps are you taking to accomplish your mission?
While there's no way to know every plan God has for you, there are some current plans you've been made aware of that you may not have completed. If so, what's keeping you from accomplishing that goal?

My thoughts:

_____

_____

_____

_____

AUGUST
DAY 10

Our eyes can play tricks on us. We see a situation occur and through the passage of time, someone may convince us that what we saw wasn't really what we saw. We tend to forget the details of what happened and allow someone else's eyes, memory or experience speak for us. You're encouraged to put your eyes back on Christ; on how He was crucified and to keep your eyes on fixed on that truth. "O foolish Galatians! Who has bewitched you that you should not obey the truth, before whose eyes Jesus Christ was clearly portrayed among you as crucified?" [Galatians 3:1] It's not enough to just know the truth, but you must keep the truth close to you. Don't allow false teachers to turn you away from what you've been taught from the very beginning.

The wisdom of knowing the truth saves you time and again from false teachers who would lead you astray.
Wisdom is based on your solid, unwavering course in walking only on God's path.

My thoughts:

_____
_____
_____
_____

AUGUST
DAY 11

The House of God is a place for people to come together to meet and fulfill deeper, more satisfying spiritual needs in their lives. It's the holy place where we meet and experience God. This is where we experience His unlimited power and supernatural authority over heaven and earth. We come to His house to worship Him; for He is the King of Kings and Lord of Lords. We each come bringing our gifts and talents ready to meet spiritual needs of His people in His house. His house should represent who He is. When we set our affections on the house of God, we make His house glorious. We make it a place where all can come and experience the presence and power of God. "Moreover, because I have set my affection on the house of my God, I have given to the house of my God, over and above all that I have prepared for the holy house, my own special treasure of gold and silver." [1 Chronicles 29:3] Set you affections on the House of God!

As God loves us conditionally, let us also bring our eternal gratitude to honor Him in His House.
Be aware of, and generously share, your blessings with others at church who also come to worship Him.

My thoughts:

_____

_____

_____

_____

AUGUST
DAY 12

Please be careful to identify God's initiatives for you, to distinguish it from your personal motives and desires. A self-centered person tends to confuse their personal agenda with God's Will. Moreover, circumstances aren't always clear to show us directions for God's leadership in our lives. Christians often talk about "open" and "closed doors," in asking God to close a door if they're not headed the right way. While it's admirable to seek indications of God's desires, the danger in this thinking lies in assuming that God's Will is always the path of least resistance (as in opening doors). Often, things may become more difficult after we try to obey God. You cannot determine if you're doing God's Will by whether or not things are going well in your current circumstances. Open or closed doors are therefore not always indications of God's directions. In seeking God's guidance, make sure that prayer, scripture and your personal circumstances all confirm the direction you sense God is leading you to. The key here is not in some formula, but that you have a trusting and faithful relationship with Him. Why? Because scripture is clear about His role working in and through us: "For it is God who is working in you, enabling you both to will and to act for His good purpose." [Philippians 2:13] Stay in the Will of God!

Our mind's unreasonable expectations can wreak havoc on spiritual experiences our hearts feel.
Tune into your heart, meditate and listen to how God wants to resolve your problems.
Never compare your situation to others, as God has different solutions for them.

My thoughts:

_____

_____

_____

_____

AUGUST
DAY 13

Burdens are weights or troubles we experience either inadvertently or are spiritually brought on into our lives. James advised: "To count it all joy" when we fall into various trials. Trials are meant to be blessings to believers because testing our faith produces patience. Patience is endurance, and endurance gives us the ability to go through trials with the confidence that it all helps produce perfection. When perfection is complete,we're purged and purified through our trials. God then fulfills and completes for us the Crown of Life that He desires to give us here on earth. [James 1:12] James also said that if we lack wisdom, we must *ask* and God will give it without reproach. In the midst of a trial, "Count it all joy." But remember to ask God for wisdom to get through it all. God will not take away our burdens summarily; we've to buckle down, work through issues and ride it out with the help of the Lord.

Why are we blessed with trials and tribulations?
That's because challenges ultimately offer lessons for ongoing
spiritual growth.
It's never too late to unlearn the old, to learn the new, in making
progress with our lives.

My thoughts:

_____
_____
_____
_____

AUGUST
DAY 14

We know the story of the three little pigs. One pig built his house with straw; another with sticks; another with brick. When the storm came, the houses of straw and sticks were blown away, but the house built with bricks withstood the storm because it was built on a firm foundation; and the inhabitants were saved. As Christians, our lives are built on the foundation that is Christ Jesus. Nothing can tear us down as long as we abide in Him. Stay rooted and grounded in Jesus, for He is the sure foundation. "And I also say to you that you are Peter, and on this rock I will build My church, and the gates of Hades shall not prevail against it." [Matthew 16:18]

When our faith is rock-solid in Christ, no momentary storms can ever blow us away from Him.
Your daily prayers and meditations on His grace and goodness are all it takes to stay grounded.
God's immortal blessings will always save us, regardless of how challenging the situation is.

My thoughts:

_____
_____
_____
_____

AUGUST
DAY 15

Everybody has a part to play in the Kingdom of God. But, also learn the wisdom of staying in your own lane. Don't compare your efforts to what other people are doing. But be inspired by what they do, so you continuously strive to offer your best efforts and labor in serving God. "I planted, Apollos watered, but God gave the increase. So then neither he who plants is anything, nor he who waters, but God who gives the increase. Now he who plants and he who waters are one, and each one will receive his own reward according to his own labor. For we are God's fellow workers; you are God's field, you are God's building." [1 Corinthians 3:6-9]

As fellow laborers working away in God's field of manifestation, we're merely instruments of a higher calling.
So it doesn't pay to compare our efforts with others' contributions.
Only soulfully offer the very best always, to please Him in His own way.

My thoughts:

_____

_____

_____

_____

AUGUST
DAY 16

When we do as the word of God instructs, He will make our way prosperous and give us good success. "This Book of the Law shall not depart from your mouth, but you shall meditate in it day and night, that you may observe to do according to all that is written in it. For then you will make your way prosperous, and then you will have good success." [Joshua 1:8]

God never intends for us to live in hardship, for His is the glory of abiding joy and abundance.
However, the human ego and mind can make it hard for us to realize God's prosperity when we desire material bling and objects that tempt us away from His path.
How will you achieve God's prosperity that's patiently waiting for you?

My thoughts:

_____

_____

_____

_____

AUGUST
DAY 17

The way to prosperity is through giving back to God unconditionally. "Give, and it will be given to you: good measure, pressed down, shaken together, and running over will be put into your bosom. For with the same measure that you use, it will be measured back to you." [Luke 6:38] This is the law of divine reciprocity. You give, and God gives in return. If you plant a good seed, it yields a harvest. Two different systems yield financially opposite results:

1) The Kingdom of God, which promotes prosperity. Jesus answered, "My kingdom is not of this world." [John 18:36]

2) The kingdom of Satan, wherein the world's system will be convicted of judgment "because the ruler of this world is judged." [John 16:11]

Renew your mind to understand what the will of God is for you, concerning your finances. Choose the better and righteous way— God's way.

If you haven't thought much about providing well for yourself and family financially, start now to ask for Him to guide you in making a new plan.
Also, begin to selflessly tithe and give back to God to show your profound gratitude.

My thoughts:

_____

_____

_____

_____

AUGUST
DAY 18

God has given us a Divine Intercessor in the Holy Spirit. [Romans 8:26,27] The Holy Spirit has an advantage over us as He already knows God's Will. Also, when He intercedes for us, He's in absolute agreement with God's Will, plus helping us know God's Will as we pray. The Holy Spirit "will not speak on His own, but He will speak whatever He hears from the Father. He'll also declare to you what is to come." [John 16:13] When praying, anticipate and be convinced the Holy Spirit already knows what God has prepared for you and wants to do with your life. That's why being able to pray in tongues is so important to believers because the Holy Spirit knows all things and connects us with the Son "who ever liveth" to intercede on our behalf. If you've not prayed in your Holy language, then from today on, take a moment to "Just do it," as Jude urges. Pray in the Holy Spirit! The Holy Spirit teaches us what we ought to pray for and assists us in our prayers. Without Him, you cannot call God your Father, nor pray with faith.

If you've not prayed in tongues, follow these simple steps for praying in freedom:
1) Because this kind of prayer takes its life and power from the Holy Spirit, you must have the Holy Spirit living inside you.
2) Accept Jesus Christ as your Lord and Savior. Once you do this, the Holy Spirit becomes a part of your life and will be in you. [John 14:16]
3) Now, you'll be able to pray in the Spirit.

My thoughts:

_____

_____

_____

_____

AUGUST
DAY 19

As citizens of the Kingdom of God, we must walk in forgiveness towards one another. Whatever causes you pain or hurt, immediately offer it to God. His way of dealing with our suffering will bring healing and peace. Jesus said we should forgive limitless times. [Matthew 18:22] This is the simple secret for keeping away: hatred, pain, bitterness, anger and resentment from lingering in our hearts. We should ask God everyday to show us who we need to forgive and who needs to be forgiven. This will free us to be all that God wants us to be. In His model prayer, Jesus told us to pray: "And forgive us our debts, as we forgive our debtors. [Matthew 6:12] Unforgiveness stops us in moving closer towards God. Christ was the perfect example of forgiveness before He died on the cross. He said: "Father forgive them, for they know not what they do," [Colossians 3:13] which put Him in a position where God could complete what He had started. Did you ask God to forgive you today? Did you forgive those who may have wounded you yesterday or the day before? If not, simply say this prayer: "Lord, I need help. I ask that you show me that which I need to be forgiven of and I forgive those who have trespassed against me. Create in me a clean heart and heal me that I may walk in your liberty for my life, In Jesus' name, Amen."

We may find it hard to forgive when we're jealous of other people who gained the upper hand after having gotten credit for our ideas.
Forgive and forget. Offer your hurts to God. He'll present you with far better opportunities for your power from Him to shine in more deserving and elevating situations. Just stay the faith.

My thoughts:

_____

_____

_____

_____

AUGUST
DAY 20

As believers, we're armed and dangerous against the enemies of God. As soldiers in the army of Christ, there are divine Rules of Engagement that we have to adhere to. Jesus called His disciples to Him and gave them "power and authority over unclean spirits to cast them out and to heal all manner of sickness and all manner of disease." [Matthew 10:1] Today, as citizens of the Kingdom, we continue to be blessed with this very same ability to cast out hostile forces and the ability to heal. We must see ourselves as soldiers in the army of the Lord to take on assignments against the enemy. First, put on the "whole armor of God." We'll be protected divinely by God while encroaching upon the enemy. We must also recognize what we're up against in the spirit and begin to "bind it." Jesus said: "No man can enter a strong man's house, and spoil his goods, except he will first bind the strong man; and then he will spoil his house."[Mark 3:27] Rule of Engagement #1 is to bind the strong man. It's very clear we must bind the enemy; meaning, to constrain with legal authority. In Matthew 16:19, Jesus gave the believer the authority to bind the devil: "And I will give you the keys of the kingdom of heaven and whatever you bind on earth shall be bond in heaven." So, use this authority to bind—to overcome depression, low self-esteem, perversion, sickness, poverty, pride and all unrighteousness. Why? Because these unwholesome traits keep you from winning in the Kingdom of God.

We're all warriors on the battlefield of life, and in constant battle with the enemy.
But, as divine aggressors protected by God's superior armor, we'll always win against the forces of darkness.

My thoughts:

_____

_____

_____

_____

AUGUST
DAY 21

Rule of Engagment #2 is to speak faith-filled words. In battling the enemy, we must be willing to engage and know we're divine aggressors who speak faith-filled words to negate the enemy and ultimately cause them to flee. Jesus used the word to resist the devil after he tried to tempt him following His forty-day fast. [Matthew Chapter 4] We have to do the same. Therefore, submit to God. Resist the devil and he will flee from you. [James 4:7] Faith-filled words are essential to successfully engage the devil in spiritual warfare. In order to bind the devil, you have to say something to him. For the word of God is living and powerful, and sharper than any two-edged sword, piercing even to the division of soul and spirit, and of joints and marrow, and is a discerner of the thoughts and intents of the heart. [Hebrews 4:12]

Speak with convincing faith to engage and then disengage the devil by forcing it to flee.
Your faith-filled words of intensity and sincerity will wither away and negate the enemy.

My thoughts:

_____

_____

_____

_____

AUGUST
DAY 22

Rule of Engagement #3 is to be aware that when we do the will of God, we may suffer temporary hardship; but we have to be willing to go through with it. You must be disciplined and willing to sacrifice in order to achieve a Kingdom result. The third and very important rule of engagement is: when battling the enemy, you must operate in the authority, in the name of Jesus Christ. Just as He gave the twelve disciples authority to cast out demons and heal all manner of sickness and disease, so has He given this authority to you. "And when He had called His twelve disciples to Him, He gave them power over unclean spirits, to cast them out, and to heal all kinds of sickness and all kinds of disease." [Matthew 10:1]

As the saying goes, no pain, no gain.
Be determined and have faith that your soul's will-power to
speak in the name of Jesus Christ will give you all the power
(plus protection) to righteously do the Will of God.

My thoughts:

_____

_____

_____

_____

AUGUST
DAY 23

Rule of Engagement #4 is to live a Holy Lifestyle, to successfully wage warfare against the devil. Paul said: "I beseech you therefore, brethren, by the mercies of God, that you present your bodies a living sacrifice, holy, acceptable to God, which is your reasonable service." [Romans 12:1] You have to live as a resident of the household of God. "He that dwells in the secret place of the most high shall abide under the shadow of the Almighty." [Psalm 91:1] As a dweller, you're a resident in God's House, and your life must be one of personal devotion to God.

Consecrate and devote your life to living totally in His grace. Blessed are the pure in heart, for their real home lies in the heart of God.

My thoughts:

_____

_____

_____

_____

AUGUST
DAY 24

Rule of Engagement #5. We are soldiers in the army of the Lord. To have ultimate victory over our adversary, the devil, you must have a consistent prayer life. The Bible encourages us to pray without ceasing. Pray until a change has taken place in your circumstances. We must be engaged in 21st century warfare, where we must be the aggressor. The Bible says we should be sober and vigilant, because the devil walks about like a roaring lion, seeking whomever he may devour. [1 Peter 5:8] Which means: 1) he's always looking for a battle and 2) he's always looking for a believer to attack and catch them off guard. So we must know these five Rules of Engagement and be ready to use them at all times. To be victorious, we have to put on the whole armor of God, bind the strong man, speak faith-filled words, operate in the authority of the name of Jesus Christ, live a holy life and maintain consistency in prayer.

Write down these Five Rules of Engagement. Memorize them. They are your divine artillery to successfully engage and vanquish the enemy—without shedding human blood and to forever instill God's word in the world consciousness!

My thoughts:

_____

_____

_____

_____

August
Day 25

There are some trials God orchestrates. Paul was painfullystruck by a thorn in his flesh. God used Satan to check on Paul, so Paul wouldn't become proud because of the divine revelations and experiences he was having in ministry. Though this thorn was a debilitating demonic attack, Paul was stoic in maintaining his apostolic ministry. Paul pleaded with God to take away the thorn. Jesus said: "My grace is sufficient for you and my strength is made perfect in weakness." [2 Corinthians 12:9] When we acknowledge God in our weaknesses and sufferings, God will enable us to come through our problems with His grace. We are much more than human conquerors fighting on life's battlefield—regardless of the burden or trial—because we can handle it with the help of the Lord.

No matter how impossibly debilitating our trials and tribulations are, know that once we divinely surrender them to God, His compassion takes over to help us heal.
God's compassion for all His children is boundless for eternity.

My thoughts:

_____

_____

_____

_____

AUGUST
DAY 26

Peter said: "Humble yourselves under the mighty hand of God, that He may exalt you in due time." [1 Peter 5:6] To get supernatural results in our walk with the Lord during times of trial, persecution, or trouble, we must first humble ourselves; so that we would be submitted to God and His perspective. No matter how long we suffer, we must maintain humility for God to deliver us and exalt us in due time. We must trust God with all our situations. That's why Peter said: "Cast all of your cares upon Him." This shows God we trust Him. Trust is faith. Without faith, it's impossible to please Him. While going through daily struggles, stresses or problems, walk in self-control and be watchful at the same time. The enemy wants us to focus on the problem—instead of exalting the Highest in us. But due to pain of suffering, many compromise with the enemy before getting to the other side, where we'll profit from our pain. It's similar to, "no pain, no gain." Everyone has to suffer to purge pain, while building character and integrity during the process. We honor and glorify Him when, with His grace, we become more perfect.

Humility is precious to develop, in humbly consecrating our lives to God.
We gain more by letting go of painful experiences when we put our trust in God—in order to transcend our imperfections, to arrive at a more exalted station in life.
In India, they say: "Let go, and let God." In what ways will you let go, to let God take over?

My thoughts:

_____

_____

_____

_____

AUGUST
DAY 27

It's difficult if not impossible to demonstrate the will of God on earth as it is in heaven, if we don't think of ourselves as truly forgiven and cleansed of past mistakes. If we hang onto false views of our mistaken identities, they effectively cancel out our potential in ministry. Some people reduce each day to: "I hope to survive." Instead, ask: "What will God do today through me?" We're created to triumphantly demonstrate the reality of the King and His Kingdom. But many of us strip down our goal to eking out a basic survival. "If I can get through the day without being depressed, without being discouraged, I will have succeeded," we tell ourselves. Our first thought of each day should instead be the reality of the Kingdom and how to manifest His mission. "His mercies are new for me every morning!" [Lamentations 3:23] Awake inspired, and know you're forgiven. Move on to newer heights of aspiration and achievement!

Learn to forgive yourself first, and it'll be easier to forgive and forget with others.
Every day, start afresh to manifest as a divine instrument, ready and eager to walk in His grace.

My thoughts:

_____
_____
_____
_____

AUGUST
DAY 28

God said: "For My thoughts are not your thoughts, and your ways are not My ways" [Isaiah 58:8] We will not carry out God's plan with our self-imposed methods. This is a basic problem people face. "We all went astray like sheep; we all have turned to our own way." [Isaiah 53:6] It is foolish to think we can accomplish God's work by using the world's methodologies and values. Such ways may seem good. We may even enjoy some moderate successes. But if we measure our success strictly by whether our numbers are growing or if we built an impressive building, we can easily assume we've been successful. While many secular organizations and other religions may be growing in numbers, buildings and wealth, they may not be pleasing God. The world says you should never commit to do anything you cannot afford. Yet God says, "Without faith, it's impossible to please Him." [Hebrews 11:6] The world values hierarchy and chains of command. God seeks to give His people one heart and mind. The world upholds the powerful, while God says, "Blessed are the meek." The world claims results are important, but God values people. When we do the work of God in our own supposed strength and wisdom, we'll never see the power of God in what we do. God reveals His way to us (such as through creativity and hard work) because those may be the only means to accomplish His purposes. When God achieves His purposes His way through us, people will come to know God, and God will be greatly glorified. People will recognize that what has happened can be explained only by the Will of God.

God's Will changes, and it's important to forsake the old to learn progressive new ways to manifest Him purposefully and righteously.

My thoughts:

_____

_____

_____

_____

AUGUST
DAY 29

Paul said: "For our light affliction, which is but for a moment, is working for us a far more exceeding and eternal weight of Glory." [2 Corinthians 4:17] Paul proclaims he, too, is experiencing pressure along with hardships. But they're nothing in view of the eternal glory that would be his when he would be in Jesus' Presence and be like Him. Paul said that all of his burdens were "light" (as in lightness in weight or easy to bear); which doesn't minimize his hardships, but allows him to see his struggles from a Kingdom perspective. "Therefore we do not lose heart. Even though our outward man is perishing, yet the inward man is being renewed day by day." [2 Corinthians 4:16]

Take heart that God hears our prayers as we struggle daily to work in his ministry, and at the workplace.
Stay focused and keep on crying like a child to be heard—so He may minister to you first, to show you His winning ways.

My thoughts:

_____

_____

_____

_____

AUGUST
DAY 30

Do the work of an Evangelist. Evangelists enable churches to go out into the communities and spread the gospel. Evangelists produce a breakthrough anointing with a transformational effect. Evangelists help with integrating new believers into the body of Christ. In Acts 8:26-40, an Angel of the Lord spoke to Philip and led him to a high-ranking Ethiopian eunuch. This man was sitting in his chariot reading the book of Isaiah. Phillip asked the man if he knew what he was reading and he replied, "How can I unless someone guides me." Phillip then preached Jesus to him. The man asked: "What hinders me from being baptized?" Phillip replied, "If you believe in your heart." And the eunuch answered: "I believe that Jesus Christ is the son of God." Both Philip and the eunuch went down into the water, and Philip baptized him. That's the real meaning of evangelism—having the ability to explain Christ to people, so they become convinced and want to walk in His glory, too.

Evangelists are an important backbone in expanding Kingdom ministry.
True evangelists inspire others not by exhorting them to convert—but in sincerely imparting the word of God in authentic, meaningful ways that make sense to them.

My thoughts:

_____

_____

_____

_____

AUGUST
DAY 31

The Lord told Abraham: "I will make you a great nation; I will bless you and make your name great; And you shall be a blessing." [Genesis 12:2] God wants you to listen carefully to His instructions as He directs you into a place of promise and prosperity. He's clear on leading you out of Egypt and away from your family. How so? Egypt represents our familiar places, bondage or a return to what we were delivered from. God wants to take us to a new place. This new place is a strategic location and a place of protection. By following His instructions, we'll find both provision and providence, as well. We'll be fruitful and our seed will be multiplied. Simply put, God promises to bless us, be with us, multiply us and make us a blessing unto others. We're tied to the blessing of Abraham. Therefore, when we follow God's instructions, He has a redemptive plan that blesses us and redeems us from the hand of the enemy.

Be courageous in listening to God's plan for you. How to?
By praying and meditating on His word to guide you to manifest
Him—wherever His will takes you to.
You will be abundantly provided for, and protected.

My thoughts:

_____

_____

_____

_____

SEPTEMBER
DAY 1

When Judas tried to betray Jesus, he could've been forgiven. But Judas instead chose to deny the Cross. We're all guilty of betraying Him in various ways. We may abandon Jesus when things get tough, or complain when things aren't going the way we'd like for them to go. What made Judas incorrigible was that he hung himself outright; he tried to pay the price for his own sin. Whenever we "hang ourselves" by carrying our own guilt and not releasing it to God, we're saying unconsciously that the Cross wasn't adequate to pay for our sins and that we must pay for it ourselves. This doesn't strengthen our resistance to sin; instead, it weakens our resolve to sin less. The messages of repentance and restoration are important to offer up as we're constantly embattled by the forces of darkness. We must not go on hanging ourselves or others, but embrace the grace of God as revealed through the Cross. "And you, being dead in your trespasses and the uncircumcision of your flesh, He has made alive together with Him, having forgiven you all trespasses." [Colossians 2:13]

Don't hang on to misdeeds and mistakes.
Offer them to God and be divinely forgiven and absolved, to start every day on a clean slate.
Before long, honest repentance and restoration become second nature to live life graciously, happily and divinely.

My thoughts:

_____

_____

_____

_____

SEPTEMBER
DAY 2

To live a God-centered life, focus on God's purposes, not your own. Try to see things from God's perspective rather than from the human point of view. Out of His infinite grace, God involves His people to accomplish His purposes. For example, God warned Noah when He was about to bring divine judgment on earth through a devastating flood. [Genesis 6:5-14] When God prepared to obliterate the debased cities of Sodom and Gomorrah, He revealed His plan to Abraham. [Genesis 18:16-21, 19:13] Likewise, God approached Gideon when He wanted to deliver the Israelites from being oppressed by the Midianite nation. [Judgment 6:11-16] When God was preparing to send the long-awaited Savior to earth, He told the teenaged girl, Mary. [Luke 1:26-38] God appeared to Saul on the road to Damascus when He was about to send the message of the gospel to Gentiles around the world. [Acts 9:1-16] The most important factor in each of these situations was: not what the individual wanted to do for God, but what God wanted to do—and how individual obedience came into play to fulfilling His goals.

Pray and meditate on God's plans for a God-centered life to bless you and your loved ones.
Divine obedience is necessary to successfully fulfill Him, and in making progress with our lives.
Divine obedience is not mindless submission, but real joy in discovering His grace—a wholesome nurturing blessing when we place our total trust in Him

My thoughts:

_____

_____

_____

_____

SEPTEMBER
DAY 3

Jesus used people as His strategy to win souls. It all started with Jesus calling upon a few chosen men to follow Him, thus revealing His evangelistic strategy. His concern was not with programs to reach the multitudes, but strategizing in reaching out to the masses with men whom the multitudes would follow. As might be expected, these early efforts of soul-winning had little or no immediate effect upon the religious life of His day. But that didn't matter greatly. As it turned out, these few early converts and apostles of the Lord were destined to become important leaders of His Church in going with Christ's Gospel to the whole world! From the standpoint of His far-ranging strategy and ultimate purpose, the significance of the lives of these original disciples would be felt throughout eternity. Now, that's smart strategy—to use committed souls to win over millions more.

In truth, we're already divinely chosen as Kingdom citizens to spread the Gospel of Truth.
Diligently seek His guidance every day to reach out to those you're meant to serve with God's word.
Write down flashes of inspiration, to better tickle your memory during the course of the day.

My thoughts:
_____
_____
_____
_____

SEPTEMBER
DAY 4

Paul exhorted in 1 Corinthians 15:58: "To be steadfast, immovable, always abounding in the work of the Lord, knowing that your labor is not in vain in the Lord." This was a time of encouragement for the saints as Paul penned this to the Corinthian Church. All of us are to be encouraged to know that as we labor in a vineyard that's ripe and ready for the picking, God rewards us for the work we do. Thus, Labor Day can be symbolic of a spiritual holiday to reflect on the work we've all accomplished in serving Christendom. And as well, look forward to the work that's ahead.

We're a dedicated team of Kingdom citizens devoted to sharing and spreading God's word. Renew your dedication to serve selflessly, every day. That's how we advance God's Kingdom. And revel in how easy and joyful it is to connect with receptive souls waiting to be reborn.

My thoughts:

_____

_____

_____

_____

SEPTEMBER
DAY 5

The Lord appointed the seventy and sent them in pairs to every place that he himself would be visiting. He unto them: "The harvest truly is great, but the laborers are few; pray ye, therefore, the Lord of the harvest, that He would send forth laborers into His harvest." [Luke 10:2] The world has more people who can be persuaded to understand and accept God's Light than ever before. However, not everyone will be receptive. Therefore, it's also possible to come out of a ripe field empty-handed. "But into whatsoever city ye enter, and they receive you not, go your ways out into the streets of the same, and say, 'Even the very dust of your city, which clingeth on (cleaveth to) us, we do wipe off against you; notwithstanding.'" [Luke 10:10-11] How do we handle rejections, given we're only human with vulnerable emotions prone to being disappointed? Never take "nos" or "yeas" personally.

Like forgiveness, non-attachment is a challenging concept to grasp and implement.
But have faith in God's compassion showing you ways of reconciling rejections, in not becoming attached to the fruits of your labor.
God experiences our efforts and gives unconditionally; so too offer your efforts in like manner.

My thoughts:

_____

_____

_____

_____

SEPTEMBER
DAY 6

We're always on the verge of tremendous breakthroughs and blessings from the Lord—and the enemy doesn't want us to receive them. But we must fight until we conquer and win! Strive to come into alignment with this clarion call to fight the forces of darkness. Begin to wage war against the enemy until we see the Hand of God prevailing. Bravely fight, to speak and declare the word of the Lord and to bind seducing spirits and the spirit of offense. May the power of God increase in you as you step up your level of commitment to defeat the enemy. With dedicated commitment, the Lord will arm and protect us in His grace as we go on the offense. The Lord will give each of us the ability to endure until the end, in Jesus' Name.

Always be fearless in taking the road less traveled to manifest God's Light.
Know that when we're committed and dedicated, God will arm and protect us divinely in every challenging situation—and we'll intuitively know what to do that's right.

My thoughts:

_____

_____

_____

_____

SEPTEMBER
DAY 7

Let us strive to be about our Father's business. When Jesus was twelve years-old, his family was returning from the Feast of the Passover in Jerusalem as they did every year. But this time, Jesus lingered in Jerusalem. When Jesus' mother realized He wasn't with them, they began to search among other family members and friends. Finally, after three days, they found Jesus. Imagine the relief that must have been. However, when confronted about his whereabouts Jesus said, "Why did you seek Me? Did you not know that I must be about My Father's business?" [Luke 2:49] Jesus was full of holy wisdom and powerful in the Spirit. He was found sitting with teachers learning the scriptures that would enable Him to minister the truth to the nation. His Father's business was to preach the gospel as shown in the great Apostolic Commission in Matthew 28:19: "Go therefore and make disciples of all the nations, baptizing them in the name of the Father and of the Son and of the Holy Spirit."

Will you be found doing the work of the Heavenly Father here on earth?
Will you be pro-active to share God's word according to the talents and skills you're blessed with?

My thoughts:

_____

_____

_____

_____

SEPTEMBER
DAY 8

Jesus is the sure way to abundant life! Businesses use various marketing slogans to try to entice consumers to use their products. They make certain statements to get consumers to buy into their claims of excellence. We all hear these slogans day in, day out: "Coca-Cola, it's the real thing." With Allstate: "You're in good hands." For Visa it's: "Everywhere you want to be." Even the US Army makes claims that you can be all you can be if you connect with them. Jesus makes multiple assertions throughout the Bible which demonstrates to us that we should try Him in walking with Him, too. His divine power has given us all things that pertain to life and godliness. 2 Peter 1:3 offers: "I am the Alpha and the Omega, the Beginning and the End." Says the Lord, "who is and who was and who is to come, the Almighty." [Revelation 1:8] "I am the way, the truth, and the life. No one comes to the Father except through Me." [John 14:6]

Delight in the beauty of walking in God's way.
His bountiful blessings shower us with opportunities to live life
happily and abundantly.

My thoughts:

_____

_____

_____

_____

SEPTEMBER
DAY 9

A most precious aspect of the Will of God is His working in and through us. He appointed and used seventy men to tell His story to men and women who did not know about Jesus. He wants to do the same through you, too, and in a greater way. Jesus said, "The Harvest is ripe." [Luke 10:1,2] Your family, co-workers, peers, colleagues and neighbors want to hear the good news of the gospel. As the 70 were sent out on a preaching campaign, so have we. Matthew 28 and Mark 16 command us: "Go into the world and preach the Gospel." Speak the word while you're out and about in the world's vineyard. Be prepared and position yourself to serve in His will. First, P.U.S.H, or Pray Until Something Happens. Then, focus on opportunities that appear. Third, God expects us to adjust and go with the flow as we become more knowledgeable of His will in our lives. Fourth, if you're involved in other less important things, drop them; reprioritize your emphasis on God's will for you. Finally, realize we've been given the tools and weapons to defeat the enemy. If it's healing that's needed, the word says you'll: "Lay hands on the sick and they will recover." [Mark 16:18] Your spiritual progress in God will intuitively show you the confidence to know that no devil can stand up to you when God is working in and through you!

Be prepared to take up arms for God—now.
Your weapons are not guns but the depth of your faith and commitment to serving Him selflessly.
God's grace is ever ready to protect and empower you, His devoted soldier!

My thoughts:

_____

_____

_____

_____

SEPTEMBER
DAY 10

Thank God He's appointed you to do His work! As "soul winners," we must have an urgency to do the work of evangelists. Soul winning is a pattern from the Old Testament: "A true witness delivers souls." [Proverbs 14:25] "The fruit of the righteous is a tree of life, and he who wins souls is wise." [Proverbs 11:30] We have a responsibility to minister to those whom God has strategically placed in our midst, to bring them divine deliverance. As trees of righteousness, we produce fruit that's inviting to the ungodly, so they eat of our good fruit, or see what good fruit looks like. Kingdom citizens are ripe for the picking for the Kingdom of God. Let someone pick and enjoy your charity, generosity, example, faithfulness and initiative for better today. It'll deliver them as you preach the gospel unto them. We're all Soul Winners!

What a privilege to be chosen to do God's work!
Show those who are hungry for the wealth of nourishment, the godly fruit of your abundance. The nature of goodness is to share with others all the very best we can offer, as in offering First Fruit.

My thoughts:

_____

_____

_____

_____

SEPTEMBER
DAY 11

In the midst of calamity, God provides a refuge. That refuge is His sanctuary where there's no need to fear or doubt. His sanctuary is a place of life, joy, peace and grace that only God can give. "There is a river whose streams shall make glad the city of God, The holy place of the tabernacle of the Most High. God is in the midst of her, she shall not be moved; God shall help her, just at the break of dawn." [Psalm 46:4-5]

The notion of "fear" is groundless, as it's an acronym for,
"False Evidence Appearing Real."
Instead, get real to discover God's awesome sanctuary where only joy, peace and love prevail.

My thoughts:

_____

_____

_____

_____

SEPTEMBER
DAY 12

The question of the day is: Who are you loyal to? Jesus said: "Let the dead bury their own dead, but you go and preach the Kingdom of God." [Luke 9:60] Loyalty to Christ takes precedence over all lesser loyalties. This word speaks to the procrastination we sometimes find ourselves in as to why we can't do something for the Lord. Whatever it is that's stopping you from being all that you should be in the Kingdom, let go of it and be determined to preach the Kingdom with your willpower!

Procrastination can throw us off our godly path in making progress with our lives.
Procrastination also prevents us from helping others make progress with their lives.
When procrastination strikes, cry even harder for Him to help you stand taller to deliver!

My thoughts:

_____

_____

_____

_____

SEPTEMBER
DAY 13

Evangelization is a process that brings the gospel to people where they are—not where you'd like them to be. When the gospel reaches people where they are, their response to gospel heralds the exciting start of a new church in a new place. It's time to expand our borders and take our minstries to new regions of the world. This great gospel must be shared abroad. "But you shall receive power when the Holy Spirit has come upon you; and you shall be witnesses to Me in Jerusalem, and in all Judea and Samaria, and to the end of the earth." [Acts 1:8]

God is always making progress and transcending His boundaries.
As children manifesting His Light, let's be confident of manifesting gospel even in unlikely places, such as meeting someone nice in the parking lot, or when traveling or shopping. And offer your experiences (happy or otherwise) back to Him to be blessed more richly.

My thoughts:

_____

_____

_____

_____

SEPTEMBER
DAY 14

We're created as new creations in Christ, that we would win over others to the Lord. And in the process, expand the Kingdom of God.We are to boldly go into the vineyard and work by sharing the good news of Jesus' death, burial and Resurrection to everyone that will hear and receive it. The fruitful harvest of our evangelistic efforts enable others to be led into a relationship with Jesus Christ and connect with a local body of like worshippers. The angels rejoice when new souls are added to the Kingdom of God through evangelism. Kingdom growth is our ultimate and true goal. [Luke 15:10] Our goal as Christians, in doing the work of evangelists, is to lead lost souls into a relationship with Jesus Christ. True growth is only accomplished by winning souls and he who wins souls is wise. [Proverbs 11:30] Be a soul winner today and every day.

What are your dreams for advancing the Kingdom?
List the ways you can evangelize fruitfully in your region.

My thoughts:

_____

_____

_____

_____

SEPTEMBER
DAY 15

Saul thought he was doing the right thing by killing Christians because they had a different viewpoint. God had to arrest Saul (Paul) to have a God moment, or a supernatural moment, that would change his life forever. Jesus said: "Saul, Saul why are you persecuting me?" [Acts 9:4] Saul had no idea what he was doing. He wasn't just killing people who believed; he'd also begun to come against the head of the church, Jesus Christ. When we live contrary to what we believe in, we also come against Him who's head of the church. Romans 12:5 proclaims: "So we, being many, are one body in Christ, and individually members of another." Christ is Head of the Church. Christ lives in us. When we use our own will, we literally persecute Him. God wanted to give Saul a God conciousness instead of a worldly one, so he wouldn't kick against the standard of the Lord. It's easy for us to kick against or compromise the standard of the Lord by allowing outside things to influence us, where we settle for something less than what God wants for us to have. This is a day to be humbled like Saul to ask: "Lord, what do you want me to do," to better know what the will of God is.

The mind can confuse and distort the soul's truth to follow God's will.
Spending quiet time to reflect and meditate on God's plan is a practical spiritual strategy, even as we spend time researching and developing projects for the home and at work.

My thoughts:

_____
_____
_____
_____

September
Day 16

Every citizen of the Kingdom should understand the importance of the word dwelling in us. To live a changed spirtual life, we must have the word of the Lord in us. "For the word of God is living and powerful, and sharper than any two-edged sword, piercing even to the division of soul and spirit, and of joints, and marrow, and is a discerner of the thoughts and intents of the heart." [Hebrews 4:12] God's Word will change us from the inside out no matter what our ouward condition may be. The eagle-eyed Prophet Isaiah said, "So shall My word be that goes forth from My mouth; It shall not return unto Me void, But it shall accomplish what I please, And it shall prosper in the thing for which I sent it." [Isaiah 55:11] Whatever God has spoken for your life, it's sure to come to pass and fulfill itself in His name. We truly live by every word from the mouth of God!

There is only one true way to know God's word for us—with prayer and meditation.
When we pray, we cry for help; when we meditate, we quiet the mind to hear God's word.
We need both wings of the soul bird to fly from inside out!

My thoughts:

_____

_____

_____

_____

SEPTEMBER
DAY 17

Both Mary and Martha were doing what the Lord had called them to do. [Luke 10:38-42] However, Martha got distracted, worried and encumbered with what Mary wasn't doing. Martha told Jesus to make Mary help her. Perhaps Martha got a little too familiar with Jesus. The Bible says Jesus was close friends with their family which made her believe she could command Jesus. Never think we can command or demand Jesus to do anything for us. He's our great high priest and He alone gives the commands. Jesus told Martha: "Mary had chosen the good part," which was to sit at His Feet to hear the word. Though Mary had been busy working, she took time to put the work of the Lord first. When working in the Kingdom of God, don't get caught mindlessly doing the work. Remember to: pray, read the Bible, fast and spend quiet time with Him.

Spend at least 10-15 minutes daily of quiet time with Him alone. Read the Bible and read the daily meditations in this book. Pray and reflect on them.
This is also time well spent to re-energize and re-balance from the day's demands.

My thoughts:
_____
_____
_____
_____

SEPTEMBER
DAY 18

Try going on a three-day fast as Saul was forced to do. This might help you understand the first steps of His will. God said in Isaiah 58:6: "Is this not the fast that I have chosen: To loose the bonds of wickedness, To undo the heavy burdens, To let the oppressed go free, And that you break every yoke?" Are there things keeping you from knowing and doing the will of God? A solution and strategy might be to sincerely consecrate your intentions. As in Verse 8: "Then your light shall break forth like the morning, Your healing shall spring forth speedily, And your righteousness shall go before you; The glory of the Lord shall be your rear guard." Ultimately, God wanted to save Saul and fill him with His Holy Spirit to begin the process of knowing and doing the will of God.

Cleansing body and spirit with periodic fasting can be a healthy and purifying good habit to get into.
But don't become extreme with fasting—learn how to fast healthily and be aware of your senses, divine and temporal.

My thoughts:

_____

_____

_____

_____

SEPTEMBER
DAY 19

Kingdom Momentum is a force released through obedience to the direction of the Holy Spirit—which always sets in motion an increase to accomplish Kingdom objectives. When God spoke creation into existence in Genesis Chapterr 1, the universe became subject to Him in being obedient to His voice. When He spoke the words, "Let there be," Kingdom momentum was set into motion. The earth was without form and void and darkness was upon the face of the deep, until God spoke the words, "Let there be." Then God created man in hHis own image and likeness. He gave male and female dominion and told them to be fruitful and multiply. Momentum continues to be established. God is still speaking and creation continues to obey His voice. To experience this Kingdom Momentum in our lives, we must also obey His voice. "If they obey and serve him they shall spend their days in prosperity, and their years in pleasure." [Job 36:11-12]

What inspires you daily to get going, to seek His word?
How do you build up your spiritual momentum every day?

My thoughts:

_____

_____

_____

_____

SEPTEMBER
DAY 20

"Evangelism is not a professional job for a few trained men, but is instead the unrelenting responsibility of every person who belongs to the company of Jesus." –Elton Trueblood

According to the scriptures, every believer has a responsibility to win souls. "Go therefore and make disciples of all nations." [Matthew 28:19] So we are to target the relationships we have as prospects for the Lord to win them over into the Kingdom of God. As you ponder this thought, God says: "He who wins souls is wise," [Proverbs 11:30] Today is a new day and in this day you should be intentional to make every effort to win someone who is lost, to return to the Lord.

Try these helpful tips for cultivating your gift of evangelism:

- Read books on personal evangelism.
- Participate in an evangelism group at your local church.
- Pray daily for those who do not know Christ.
- Look for the daily opportunities to have a conversation about your faith...
- Spend time with people outside of church.

What are some practical ways you can overcome your fears of reaching out to strangers?
Such as offering a: heartfelt smile, warm handshake or saying 'hello' first?

My thoughts:

_____
_____
_____
_____

SEPTEMBER
DAY 21

Giving is a pattern that was established in the Old Testament, and is still fashionable today. Scripture is very clear that if you're going to get God to move today, you have to give of your self, substance and service. Paul said: "He who sows to his flesh will of the flesh reap corruption, but he who sows to the Spirit will of the Spirit reap everlasting life." [Galatians 6:8] God expected Israel to give, even in difficult times. Though locusts were eating up and destroying their crops and goods, and drying up what they had, God still commanded they bring Him a tenth of all they had labored for. Then He said He would: "Open windows to them, Pour out blessings that overtake them, Rebuke the devourer for their sake, and the vine would not fail them in the field." [Malachi 3:10-11] In knowing His will, we must do all we can to show Him our love and trust in His way for us.

As God is kind and generous to us, let's not forget to show our gratitude with generous offerings, as well.
Tithing is one way to give of our best to show our appreciation of His grace.
Giving from the heart's generosity always trumps forking over large sums of money for people's recognition.

My thoughts:

_____

_____

_____

_____

SEPTEMBER
DAY 22

Let the Word of Christ dwell richly in you. It's a matter of life or death. God gave each of us the ability to choose life or death. It's not His will for anyone to perish or die, separated from Him, to spend eternity with the devil. Life is eternity with God, death is to live in eternity unseparated from God. The Bible is very clear for Life with God will bring us good—while life without God brings evil. [Deuteronomy 30:19] God is crying out to us as He did to Moses and the children of Israel: "Choose ye this day whom you will live for, God or the devil, heaven, or hell, which will it be?" [Deuteronomy 30:11-20]

The choice is clear—heaven or hell, for more peace of mind and eternal salvation.
Spending eternal life with God is a no-brainer, so always walk in His word.

My thoughts:
_____
_____
_____
_____

SEPTEMBER
DAY 23

Will a man rob God? [Malachi 3:8] That was the question God asked the Israelites when they fell out of doing His will. The Israelites were God's chosen people for whom He had come into covenant with. He reminded them: "I am the Lord, who changes not." [Malachi 3:6] That's because they lived another life outside of the will of God. God loves us so much and is always faithful to His word that He finds ways to bring us back to Him. He said to the Israelites, "Return to me, and I will return to you." [Malachi 3:7] In other words, repent of your wayward ways so that our relationship can be reestablished. For they had been out of fellowship with God for a long time. Malachi Chapter 3 reported that they experienced God's retributive judgment. Because they had opted for another life, God allowed locusts to eat up and destroy what they had. Because they stopped giving their service, substance and of themselves, God challenged them to repent and to come back into a right relationship with Him through His final Old Testament covenant. Many of us have missed it with God because we stopped giving with heartfelt tithing and offerings. God can turn around situations to set our feet back on solid ground—if we remember to give to Him, too.

As God is good and generous to us, let us repay His kindnesses with whatever we can offer from the heart.
We can fundraise, donate money and volunteer to help expand our Kingdom, in as many creative ways that bring us joy.
Ways that bring you joy will zing up your giving more meaningfully for both giver and recipient.

My thoughts:

_____
_____
_____
_____

SEPTEMBER
DAY 24

Jesus said: "Go out into the highways and hedges, and compel them to come in, that My house may be filled." [Luke 14:23] We're empowered to preach the gospel and to take authority over the enemy. Wherever God has you strategically located at this moment, it's your responsibility to compel the lost to be saved. As Peter was evangelizing in his region, he crossed the path of Aeneas (who had been bedridden for eight years and was paralyzed). God used Peter to speak healing into Aeneas' life— which brought about a miraculous healing witnessed by others. Because Peter allowed God to use him, he became a conduit for the manifestation of God. Peter told Aeneas to do what he couldn't do for eight years: "Arise and make up your bed." Be prepared to meet someone today who has been paralyzed with rebellion, depression, rejection, unforgiveness or an additive behavior. They need you to minister to them. Whatever the concern, Jesus said: "The works that I do you will do also, and greater works than these will you do." Do the will of the Father today and divinely complete His work. It's Harvest Time!

Be prepared and ready to carry out God's work at any moment. Be an inspiration to everyone you meet. Your goodness will touch their hearts, and they'll pass it along to yet others along the way.
The nature of goodness is always to share, while spreading an intangible God power.

My thoughts:

_____

_____

_____

_____

SEPTEMBER
DAY 25

No matter how you look at it, ultimately your security lies in the Lord. In John 10:28 Jesus said: "And I give them eternal life, and they shall never perish; neither shall anyone snatch them out of my hand." As believers in Christ, we're guaranteed eternal life if we hear the voice of the Lord and follow Him. No matter what happens in life, nothing can snatch us away, because He promises to cover and protect us. So go about your day knowing that no weapon formed against you will ever pierce through because our Father in Heaven is greater than all. He's greater than the trial you're experiencing, greater than the need that you have, greater than the financial problems you have, greater than your marital issues, greater than anything or anyone. Jesus knows His followers. When we cast our cares over to Him, He works everything out for our good. Keep standing in Him and don't let outside voices cause you to change your dedicated disposition in Him.

Our ultimate security lies in trusting God, always!
No matter what storms may blow your way, be steadfast in Him.
Simply offer up your problems. Remember to "let go, and let God."

My thoughts:

_____

_____

_____

_____

SEPTEMBER
DAY 26

We're all out in battle at this present dispensation. There's a heavy assault from the enemy against the churches of God to make you quit, give up and throw in the towel on what God said He would do for this year. So, just counter with your own assault. Be on the offensive. Paul said: "Therefore take up the whole armor of God that you may be able to withstand in the evil day, and having done all, to stand." [Ephesians 6:13] Start interceding against the negative spirits until you see the manifestation of the Lord. Everyone needs to pray and not faint. If you feel you're wavering, connect with another Christian soldier who can help you to be strengthened for the battle. We're in this battle to win it. This is the evil day that was spoken of prophetically that we must now stand up against, and fight!

Please never see yourself as fighting the enemy alone.
The church is empowered and powerful; seek the counsel of
church Elders and godly men and women who are ready anytime
to lend their support.
You only have to ask, and it shall be given, in the Lord's Name.

My thoughts:

_____

_____

_____

_____

SEPTEMBER
DAY 27

You need a plan! God has devised a plan, much like a blueprint, for each of us to prosper and to enjoy good success into our future. [Jeremiah 29:11] It's up to us to know the plan, understand it and carry it out faithfully to experience God's intended blessings. We must write down the vision and make it plain. [Habakkuk 2:2] Write down what the Holy Spirit is showing you for your life's sake, so that it's indelibly branded into the recesses of your mind and at the forefront of your consciousness. The plan may not be for this very moment or day, but may be for an appointed future time. Writing it down will make it seen for generations to come. If there's no plan or you can't articulate it, there'll be confusion about where God is leading you. This may ultimately lead to destruction. Solomon said, "Where there is no vision, the people perish." [Proverbs 29:18] But where there's a plan, you have a strategy to defeat the enemy. When you have a plan, you can achieve breakthrough results with prayer. With a plan, you can see victory! Write it down and make it plain and simple. Everyone needs a plan.

A student in school learns to develop a career plan to graduate and for professional success.
A spiritual student (at any age) needs a plan too, for ongoing spiritual progress in successfully defeating the enemy.

My thoughts:

_____
_____
_____
_____

SEPTEMBER
DAY 28

How many souls have you won to the Lord this week? How many people have you prayed for this week? How many people experienced the love of God through your ministry this week? How many people did you lay hands on and they recovered spiritually and emotionally, if not physically, this week? Ultimately, each one of us is responsible for taking action. Wherever it is that the Lord has strategically placed us to serve Him in other people. Jesus said, "I came to save the Lost." [Luke 19:10] Now that we've been saved by our gracious Lord, we should also have this same passion that Jesus had to win over and love the lost at any cost.

Reflect on how your personal ministry has touched others.
What did you give that moved them the most?
What can you offer more of next time?

My thoughts:

_____
_____
_____
_____

SEPTEMBER
DAY 29

There are still millions of seats God needs to fill at His banquet table for the wedding of His Son. When the ones who had received the wedding invitation made excuses as to why they couldn't come, Father God became very angry. He said to His servants (the saints): "The wedding is ready, but those who were invited were not worthy. Therefore go into the highways, and as many as you find, invite to the wedding supper, the Lord said." [Matthew 22:8-9] In Luke's narrative of this wedding supper, the Lord said: "Go out quickly into the streets and lanes of the city, and the servant said, 'Master, it is done as you commanded, and still there is room.'" Then the Master said to the servant, "Go out into the highways and hedges, and compel them to come in, that My house may be filled." [Luke 14:21-23] Keep compelling them to come and celebrate!

God's work is ongoing to touch millions more people to
recognize and celebrate His word. Never give up on your
passionate ministry to compel more to attend and heartily eat of
His heavenly feasts, so they too can be nourished eternally.

My thoughts:

_____

_____

_____

_____

SEPTEMBER
DAY 30

Knowing and doing the will of God enables Kingdom citizens to walk in a place called liberty. Liberty means to be free. God wants us to be free of our demons so we're able to render unto Him a seed that will cause Him to move to turn around our situations. When we're bound, we operate in fear instead of in faith. Paul told Timothy: "God never gave us a spirit of fear, but of power, of love, and of a sound mind." [2 Timothy 1:7] Fear causes us to be timid or apprehensive in giving of ourselves, substance and service unto God. As God's people, debts shouldn't dictate to us how we live our lives. Jesus said: "I came to give you life, and life more abundantly." The widow in 1 King 17:8-16 was in a tight financial bind. All she could see was herself and her son eating the last of what they had, then dying. But God repositioned her for a major turn around simply with a word from Elijah the Prophet. "Believe in His Prophet and so shall you prosper." [2 Chronicles 20:20] She trusted in the word and sowed a seed from out of her need to receive a bountiful turnaround. Don't let what you don't have just now, or a lack, keep you from eating and being nourished from faith in God.

Faith in God saves all, and even moves mountains.
Ask: How strong is my faith and how can I keep on watering it?
What seeds would you like to plant at the end of this month, to perhaps see results next month, or by year's end?

My thoughts:

_____

_____

_____

_____

OCTOBER
DAY 1

There are two kinds of believers in each local church, "milk believers" and "wine believers." Milk believers do real well at first. But add time, and they become soured and spoiled. Worse, milk believers are not satisfied to spoil by themselves, they also sour others. Be on the lookout. However, wine believers just get better with time. The longer they're around gospel teachings, the richer, smoother and more mature they become. In the process of time, God allows all believers to go through testings, to better develop endurance and divine fortitude in them. Don't allow these tests to offend you or make you bitter. Let the proving ground of God reveal the endurance that's needed to keep you running in the race with patience and gratitude.

At the first sign of milk believers diluting our pool of wine believers, be sure to tell an Elder.
This is not snitching, but a conscious act to preserve our Kingdom's integrity for every member.

My thoughts:

_____

_____

_____

_____

OCTOBER
DAY 2

Ministry is always shifting from glory to more glory to even more glory. Yet God says, "I am the Lord, I change not." As we shift and move in sharing His glory, we must maintain ourselves in the Holy Ghost, righteousness and in the faith. Continue to keep seeking God for more of His purpose to bless your life. We're in the high season of our lives where doors of opportunity are plentiful; thus increase is inevitable. We're in the fall season where things begin to turn a beautiful color—yet fall off in time. Many things change color in our lives. As colors brighten up, they shine a light on us as Christians. We're the light of the world. Let your light shine, that many more are won over to the Lord; not only now, but forever.

When you sparkle forth your light, everyone notices how positive and cheerful you are.
In what ways would you like to shine even more brightly this season?

My thoughts:

_____

_____

_____

_____

OCTOBER
DAY 3

Paul said: "Know this, that in the last days perilous times will come." [2 Timothy 3:1] He was speaking prophetically to Timothy about the future, and the times we're in now. Have you wondered about our world today, and what's going on? Such as: murders, rapes, shootings, violence, poverty, drugs, hate crimes, young people rising up against their parents and all sorts of nasty things that reflect our living in perilous times? We're in a war much like the Iraq war—except that ours is a spiritual assault. The people of God must rise up and be delivered from the very tactics the enemy is using against us. We must be battle-ready with the proper divine armor and spiritual weapons to fight the enemy. And we must engage ourselves as soldiers in the army of the Lord. This fight is fixed and we always win! This is our harvest season! If you've been planting seed this year, it's time to reap what you've sown. Reach out to those who have received your ministry and invite them to church with you. Go get your harvest and celebrate!

The souls of those who respond to your ministry will be forever grateful for your help to see the light.
They're your delightful and eternal rewards for planting seeds and harvesting them in due time.

My thoughts:

_____

_____

_____

_____

OCTOBER
DAY 4

God's plan is for us to be blessed. He places a desire in everyone's heart to strive for better through the peace we obtain by knowing Him. [John 14:27] Remember Eve in the garden? She ate of the fruit and then gave it to Adam, and helped usher in the fall of man. She was enticed by the thought of being better by the promises of the serpent. The devil deceived her and caused her to veer off track from God's plan for her life; and ultimately for all mankind, simply because she wanted better. As we see here, the world's way to better will end in destruction—but God's way to better will end in peace and joy in the Lord. God has so much He wants to prosper us with. Malachi 3 says that when we give of our increase, He will pour us out such a blessing that we won't have room to receive it all. The abundance of God is never ending. His desire for His people is for us to walk in the fullness of His prosperity. Make sure your spiritual life is in the center of God's will and God's plan. When your life is in alignment with the will of God, things start to happen. Everything and everyone around you becomes blessed. "Blessed is everyone who fears the Lord, Who walks in His ways." [Psalm 128:1]

God wants us to be blessed better, to live in His prosperity and never-ending abundance.
We only have to be focused on His Bounty—not on external modes of material gains.

My thoughts:

_____

_____

_____

_____

OCTOBER
DAY 5

Paul makes it clear the work of the ministry is spiritual warfare. It's not warfare after the flesh. We're fighting spiritual enemies for spiritual purpose and therefore must use spiriutal weaponry. The word says that although we walk in the flesh, we don't war according to the flesh. The weapons of our warfare are not carnal but might in God; these weapons are used for pulling down strongholds against the church. Our weapons are used for casting down arguments and everything that exalts itself against the knowledge of God. And to bring every thought into holy captivity unto the obedience of Christ. [2 Corinthians 10:3-5] Strongolds are faulty thinking patterns based on lies and deception. Deception is one of the primary building block weapons of the devil used in building strongholds. Strongholds cause us to mentally revolt that block us from God's best. How do we recognize strongholds? Through the grace of discernment and detection—with prayer and meditation.

Be spiritually vigilant against those who would cast negative thoughts and arguments on your faith. Just avoid these people; this is the easiest way to not invite perdition into your life.
Be even stronger and more determined to pray and meditate for God's true guidance to bless you when you come across these folks.

My thoughts:

_____

_____

_____

_____

OCTOBER
DAY 6

Problems created by our inner demons include: emotional, mental, speech, sexual, addictions, physical infirmities and religious error. Invoke these seven qualities to be delivered. 1) Honesty. "Search me, O God, and know my heart: try me, and know my thoughts; and see if there be any wicked way in me, and lead me in the way everlasting." [Psalm 139:23,24] 2) Humility. "God resisteth the proud, but giveth grace unto the humble. Submit yourselves therefore to God." [James 4:6,7] 3) Repentance. "The time is fulfilled, and the Kingdom of God is at hand. Repent, and believe in the gospel." [Mark 1:15] 4) Renunciation. "O generation of vipers, who hath warned you to flee from the wrath to come, bring forth fruits therefore meet for repentance." [Matthew 3:7,8] 5) Forgiveness. "For if ye forgive men their trespasses, your Heavenly Father will also forgive you: But if ye forgive not men their trespasses, neither will your Father forgive your trespasses." [Matthew 6:14,15] 6) Prayer. "Whosoever shall call upon the name of the Lord shall be delivered." [Joel 2:32] 7) Warfare. "Be strong in the Lord, and in the power of his might. Put on the whole armour of God, that ye may be able to stand against the wiles of the devil." [Ephesians 6:10-12]

These timeless spiritual qualities are also practical with family, friends and in the workplace.
Honesty, humility, forgiving easily, repenting, prayer and warfare always save us.

My thoughts:

_____

_____

_____

_____

OCTOBER
DAY 7

As Kingdom citizens, we must learn to keep ourselves in the love of God. This is the Will of God for those who dedicate our lives to the Lord. Jude admonished the Church to: "Build themselves up on your Holy faith" and to pray in the Holy Spirit" to maintain the standard that we know God wants us to live. [Jude 1:20] It's a challenge to be consistent in not being influenced by the non-aspiring, unspiritual world. This was the dilemma Jude faced while leading the people of his day. The Church was infiltrated by false teachers which led them to live other than what had been taught. Jude proclaimed: "We have to contend for the faith;" because losing your faith means losing everything else that goes with it. Every believer must have faith in God. "The just shall live by faith." [Romans 1:17] As Kingdom people, we must fight like the boxer-fighters of old: Sony Liston, Joe Frazier, Hit Man Hearns, Sugar Ray Leonard and the legendary Muhammad Ali. They were knocked down while competing, but still consistently maintained their championship charisma.

We can also be consistent and charismatic in walking with the Lord.
Be inspired by these boxer heroes; even your neighbor—by anyone who consistently extols God.

My thoughts:

_____

_____

_____

_____

OCTOBER
DAY 8

In the book of Luke, Anna was a prophetess and a great example of someone who honors God day in, day out. "And this woman was a widow of about eighty-four years, who did not depart from the temple, but served God with fastings and prayers night and day." [Luke 2:37] The fasts that you present to the Lord should always represent honor for God in selfless servitude.

Who inspires you with their selfless actions?
Make a list of these people.
Figure out why they're great examples and heroes to you, in their honoring God.

My thoughts:

_____

_____

_____

_____

OCTOBER
DAY 9

In demolishing the enemy, step up to fight even more effectively. "Some will depart the faith giving heed to deceiving spirits and doctrines of demons." [1 Timothy 4:1] Apostasy causes believers to deny essential Christian doctrines. Paul warned to bind devil demons so they wouldn't influence those in households of faith. Signs are: believers staying home from church, in taking their soul salvation lightly. We live in perilous times with increasing rape, murder, pornography and poverty. It's easy to succumb, to be destroyed and prevented from seeing the King. "Jesus will return for the church without spot or wrinkle." For us to be that pristine church, we must beat the devil at his tactics. How? First, be determined to resist regardless of what happens. Second, use your sword of the spirit as Jesus did when the devil attempted to deceive Him. Know our word and use it against the enemy's tactics. Jesus successfully resisted the devil, making him flee. [Luke 4:3-13] Arise, and defeat the devil with the sword of the spirit! Walk in the same victory Jesus did! Continue to bind the enemy because he's already a defeated foe!

We must invoke our soul's willpower to fearlessly and fiercely defeat the enemy.
It's important to also know the word, to more effectively use the sword of the spirit.

My thoughts:

_____
_____
_____
_____

OCTOBER
DAY 10

When Paul was at the end of his ministry, he charged Timothy to do the work of an evangelist. [2 Timothy 4] This was a serious responsibility because Paul charged him before God and Jesus Christ. Remember when we were kids, we used to say: "I double-dog dare you to do it?" Paul impressed upon Timothy that he had to have an urgency about his ministry; and to call upon his life because God will judge the living and the dead at His appearing. Paul said: "Preach the word in season or out of season with all long suffering and teaching." Timothy was exhorted to refute the false fables that had infiltrated the church. Paul said: "Be watchful, endure afflictions and fulfill your ministry." In other words: know what's happening around your sphere of influence and prepare for rejection because some may have turned their ear away. We must always remain diligent and faithful to the call of God, for there are people who shall be won to the Lord.

Start being committed to take up your responsibility to minister. Be serious about this great charge—which is a divine privilege to minister to others, while remaining faithful to God.

My thoughts:

_____

_____

_____

_____

OCTOBER
DAY 11

If you have faith, nothing shall be impossible to you. Christ said to the disciples: "Because you have so little faith. Truly I tell you, if you have faith as small as a mustard seed, you can say to this mountain, 'Move from here to there,' and it will move. Nothing will be impossible for you." [Matthew 17:20] Faith is needed to demonstrate our trust in God. [Hebrews11:1] Faith is the substance of things hoped for, the evidence of things not seen. Faith gives us the assurance to the things that we have hope for and convinces us to believe in things we have never seen. Our salvation comes through faith. It is by grace that we have been saved through faith. [Ephesians 2:8-9] Faith pleases God. He rewards those who diligently seek Him. "Supernatural things happen when asked in faith." [Matthew 21:21] Have faith in God and seek Him daily in prayer to experience breakthroughs in all areas of your life. Ask in faith, and according to His will, He will do whatsoever you ask. [John 14:14] Act on faith and walk by faith—to receive eternal life.

Abiding faith is the bedrock of consistency and confidence in living according to God's will.
Faith moves us deeply with belief—to believe in His word about things we can't see.

My thoughts:

_____

_____

_____

_____

OCTOBER
DAY 12

Demons desire to dwell in human bodies and exercise their control while wreaking havoc on us. Different parts of the body provide prime dwelling places for various demonic spirits. For example, stubbornness and rebellion can lodge in the neck and shoulder areas. Spirits of lust can dwell in the eyes, hands, abdomen and any part of the body that easily yields to sexual sinning. Spirits of mind control, fear and confusion dwell in the head. Pride can lodge in the back and spine. Spirits of infirmity lodge in the body too, and must be cast out before physical, emotional and spiritual healing can take place. Jesus loosened the spirit of infirmity dwelling in a woman's back and spine areas, and healed her by casting the infirmity out of her. [Luke 13:11-13]

Even medical science acknowledges the mind-body connection in bringing about healing.
It's important to remain positive while facing physical challenges, as this makes it easier to heal.
Pray hard for the Holy Spirit to make you whole according to His Will

My thoughts:

_____

_____

_____

_____

OCTOBER
DAY 13

The Lord wants to raise up believers to become leaders in every sphere of society. We cannot fold our hands and think our prayers will convert every leader into a godly person. We can't blindly hope that God will raise up good leaders from out of nowhere. Nope! Truly, we're the agents of spiritual change. We must actively raise up God-fearing and God-loving leaders from our own ranks to impart their spiritual impact on society.

As agents of spiritual change, we must step up to befriend potential leaders, and cultivate their godly service for the good of society.
Spiritual discipline for Kingdom citizens requires true dedication to the cause—even in recognizing good leaders who would grow God's kingdom.

My thoughts:

_____

_____

_____

_____

OCTOBER
DAY 14

The question of the day is, "Why Worry?" Medical professionals identify both good and bad stress. Small amounts of stress are good, but extreme or long-term stress will cause your body to wear down quickly, thus leading to health or mental problems. Examples of short-term stresses are: what you feel before an important job interview, a test, presentation or sporting event. Long-term stress is constant worry over your job, school or family—which perpetually drains your energy and ability to perform effectively. Jesus asked: "Which of you worrying can add one cubit to his stature?" [Matthew 6:27] Worry can become serious distractions. Worry breeds four things: anxiety, fear, dread and apprehension. Dread will cause you to wake up every morning hating to go to work. Apprehension will cause you to be slow to do something or be stuck in your tracks. God wants us to trust Him as we walk out our destiny in Him. Solomon exhorted: "Trust in the Lord with all your heart, and lean not to your own understanding. In all your ways acknowledge Him and He shall direct your paths." [Proverbs 3:5]

Why worry? Instead, place all your trust in God. Your petitions will be heard.
But don't expect God to answer them according to your desires. God does the needful according to His Will and Hour.

My thoughts:

_____

_____

_____

_____

OCTOBER
DAY 15

As soul winners and cultivators of the faith, know too that we can be afflicted by others. Paul said: "Endure afflictions like a good soldier." [2 Timothy 2:3] People will talk about us, separate themselves from us and even kick us to the curb. But eventually, everything will be all right because when we endure to the end, Jesus said that we "will be saved." [Matthew 10:22] Regardless of whether we're reviled or hated, we must continue to do the work that God has assigned to every believer. The goal of this important work is to win souls—not succumb to ungodly criticism and ignorant forces.

Spiritual discipline requires we aspire to our highest in sharing His light—by winning souls.
How will you emotionally detach from unfounded comments from non-believers?

My thoughts:

_____

_____

_____

_____

OCTOBER
DAY16

We have commanded every fowl and demonic spirit to depart in the name of Jesus! They must go! When Paul and his evangelistic team were confronted by a girl who was possessed with a spirit of divination, he became annoyed by this spirit. [Acts 16:16-18] We should be rightly annoyed by any unwholesome spirit following us. Paul allowed this spirit to only go so far before he decided to do an exorcism. He commanded the demon to come out of the girl and to go away, forever. As you confront the strongholds of: seduction, offence, rebellion and division, command them to manifest. Then take authority over them and command them to go from our region. Each of us have been set up in strategic places to fight the devil. Let's all be unified in our efforts. Take time today to participate in warfare prayer to put on your armor and wage war against the enemy of our souls. When Paul did this, the demon came out that very hour. Today, this is the hour for the devil to come out, in Jesus' Name.

Take up spiritual arms to cast out the forces of darkness and demonic behavior in your region.
Your deep faith is God's proud armor protecting you every step of the way!

My thoughts:

_____

_____

_____

_____

OCTOBER
DAY 17

"You know that the rulers of the Gentiles lord it over them, and those who are great exercise authority over them. Yet it shall not be so among you; but whoever desires to become great among you, let him be your servant." [Matthew 20:25-26] The service you give for others qualifies you for increase and elevation in the Kingdom of God. There are a number of ways to serve God by serving others. These include: what you do for your family, volunteering in the community, giving your tithes and offerings into your local church, having compassion on others and being hospitable, to list a few. The Bible instructs us to serve wholeheartedly, as if we were serving the Lord, not people. [Ephesians 6:7] A divine partnership with God is established by service to someone else.

There is greatness and goodness in serving others, even as God serves us so lovingly.
Offer your love and serve selflessly and wholeheartedly—without expectation of return.
God will love and serve you with His divine increase, His way.

My thoughts:

_____
_____
_____
_____

OCTOBER
DAY 18

To be Kingdom-minded is to reflect the world's thinking and philosophy and to shift to live by superior principles from a superior place. The Kingdom to which Christians belong is superior. The principles we live by are also superior. Love is superior to hatred. Mercy is superior to vengeance. Honesty is superior to dishonesty. These are some of the weapons we use in our promised lands as we cast our swords of faith. This world can only be properly managed by people who rule from a superior place with superior principles. Only good can overcome evil; this is one of the most important spiritual laws. Paul admonished: "Do not be overcome by evil, but overcome evil with good." [Romans 12:21] Remember, God is more powerful than anything you may know!

Kingdom citizens live by divinely superior principles proclaimed from a superior place.
Always remember God is more powerful than anything you may ever know!
Repeat this affirmation often to calm down; even more intensely, when in trouble.

My thoughts:

_____

_____

_____

_____

OCTOBER
DAY 19

The life of Mary and Martha are studies in contrasts. Jesus saw the best in Mary and how she responded to the Lord. Martha though, was caught up in serving house guests and didn't take time to sit and hear the teachings of the Lord as He ministered to the disciples. Mary and Martha were both disciples and spiritually gifted. The game-changer for Mary was that she listened to the word—while Martha, being distracted by the work at hand, didn't. In serving the Lord, He must be involved and be a part of the equation. Four things set Mary apart form Martha. Mary humbled herself before the Mighty Hand of God. She worshipped the Lord in spirit and in truth. If that wasn't enough, she became a servant unto Him. And she heard the word. [Luke 10:38-42]

It's important to learn the art of listening for everyday living.
Kingdom citizens must be impelled to listen carefully to the
Lord's word.
How do you listen carefully while conversing?

My thoughts:

_____

_____

_____

_____

OCTOBER
DAY 20

Deliverance is an essential part of our preparation for the Bride of Christ to get rid of "spots" and "wrinkles." Since the Church for which Christ is to be "holy and without blemish," unclean spirits must be purged from our lives. Is this cleaning to be a sovereign act of the Lord, or does it involve responsibility on the part of the believer? The word says: "Let us be glad and rejoice, and give honor to Him: the marriage of the Lamb is come, and His wife hath made herself ready." [Revevelations 19:7] This verse emphasizes our human responsibility to be pure and clean, both inside and out. We must make ourselves ready for the coming of the Lord. Some seem to think that waiting for the Lord's coming is a time when great change will automatically take place, when all their deficiencies will instantly and miraculously be remedied. But, this is far from the truth! God uses His word to prepare us for the arrival of Jesus Christ. We must take that word and put it into action by actively doing what it takes to prepare for His arrival.

We must be proactive and dynamic in becoming godly. No pain, no gain.
Cleanliness is next to godliness for body, mind and spirit.
Clean up your act now, to prepare for His arrival!

My thoughts:

_____

_____

_____

_____

OCTOBER
DAY 21

Remain steadfast and immovable in the Lord as you press for your breakthrough this week. Like Jehoshaphat and Judah, we too must continue with our strategy of consecrating ourselves for the betterment of our community, families and ourselves. Wake up, arise and mobilize your efforts so that the unity we walk in will cause us to break out in joyful song and celebratory dancing, for our enemies to be defeated. Stay rooted and grounded in prayer.

Loving and serving God is a joyful experience. It's the inner delight every true believer experiences that defies explanation. Consecrate all you do to this higher cause for self, others and community.
List some of the ways that inspire you to start, now.

My thoughts:

_____

_____

_____

_____

OCTOBER
DAY 22

Jesus said, "And this gospel of the Kingdom shall be preached in all the world for a witness unto all nations; and then shall the end come." [Matthew 24:14] Our mandate is to take the gospel of the Kingdom to the whole world, not only in word but also in demonstration with worthy actions. When we demonstrate the goodness of God, His goodness draws people to repentance, which then brings them into the Kingdom of God. Preach the Word!

Preach the Word with your actions, too.
What have you done to share His Word?
How will you continue preaching with worthy actions?

My thoughts:

_____

_____

_____

_____

OCTOBER
DAY 23

It's encouraging to hear so many inspiring testimonies on how the Lord was sustained with your selfless deeds! Keep on pressing today and every day, as you devotedly seek God for your ongoing spiritual growth and progress. There are so many things God wants to do through us and He also wants to do things for us. God said that He's "a very present help in the time of trouble." [Psalm 46:1] With all that's going on around us, we can say that trouble is always present. But God, our Deliverer, brings us safely through it all.

With the flux of life challenging us regionally and around the world, it's easy to lose perspective and the confidence that problems can be resolved.
But honoring God as a palpable Presence in our consciousness guiding us every step of the way, saves the day, every day.

My thoughts:

_____

_____

_____

_____

OCTOBER
DAY 24

God has given a great command in 1 Thessalonians 5:18: to be thankful at all times for all of the wonderful things He has done for us. Scripture teaches us to give thanks in everything, for this is the will of God in Christ Jesus concerning you. Though your days may sometimes be difficult and situations may arise that are hard to handle, God still encourages us to continue to give thanks. James said to "count it all joy when ye fall into various trials." [James 1:2] Express your gratitude for all the Lord has done while you were in the midst of a trial. "O give thanks unto the Lord, for He is good: for His mercy endureth forever." [Psalm 107:1] No matter how bleak your path appears momentarily, God is still good in guiding you through the experience. Just choose to have a positive attitude and live in the joy the Lord has promised to his good and faithful servants.

If you haven't begun a journal of thanks, today is the day to start one.
List 10 things you're most grateful for, today.
Continue listing 10 things (people, events, etc.) every day, here on out.

My thoughts:

_____

_____

_____

_____

OCTOBER
DAY 25

Stay rooted and grounded in prayer to remain focused on things the Lord wants to show you. We must seek God in this season for tactical reasons to welcome the New Year that's only two months away. Praise God today for the breakthroughs that you have been blessed to receive. Keep pressing for the high calling of serving Christ Jesus. "Brethren, I do not count myself to have apprehended; but one thing I do, forgetting those things which are behind and reaching forward to those things which are ahead, I press toward the goal for the prize of the upward call of God in Christ Jesus." [Philippians 3:13-14]

Prayer helps us stay focused and grounded in our spiritual discipline.
A practical way to incorporate prayer into a busy work day is to take 1-10 minute prayer breaks.
Say, a minute behind the wheel before driving off, and another minute in gratitude for your safe arrival.
How else can you integrate smaller, intense and prayerful moments into your everyday activities?

My thoughts:

_____

_____

_____

_____

OCTOBER
DAY 26

Accountability is responsibility shown to another for doing an activity well. It's also described as the trait of being answerable to someone, for something; or being responsible for one's conduct. It's a Kingdom concept embraced by all because of the unique benefits for everyone. When you know someone will periodically check in on you, it'll motivate you to do better. You'll also begin to have a different view of those in authority, when you become answerable to someone else. This viewpoint will begin putting you in line for greater responsibility, even set you up for promotion. Being accountable to God will challenge you to maintain godly characteristics set forth by the fruit of the Spirit: love, joy, peace, long suffering, gentleness, goodness, faith, meekness, temperance. [Galatians 5:22-23] Sustainability means to keep in existence, and maintain consistency and continuity. Without accountability, you'll have limited sustainability. Without sustainability, you'll achieve little long-term impact. These attributes increase your ability to serve selflessly. [James 5:16] Confess you trespasses to one another that you may be healed. The fervent prayers of a righteous person avails much effectiveness to everyone.

How will you step up to the plate in church with your talents and skills?
How will you sustain your accountability for this week, for next month and the entire year?

My thoughts:

_____
_____
_____
_____

OCTOBER
DAY 27

The Bible speaks of having discipline in every area of our lives. "And those who belong to Christ Jesus have crucified the flesh with its passions and appetites and desires." [Galatians 5:24,25] If we live by the Holy Spirit, let us also walk by the Spirit. Discipline is one of the hardest things to grasp and maintain. Being an athlete for most of my youth to young adult years, I had to become disciplined to develop a culture to win. I had to prepare myself mentally and physically, while building up strength, endurance and skill to be good at the sport I was in, whether track, football, basketball or wrestling. I always started the game, match or race with the intention of winning. I had this mindset in the natural. We must have this same mindset in the spiritual. We must discipline ourselves in our times of prayer, fasting, worship and meditating on the word of God. "Know ye not that they which run in a race run all, but one receiveth the prize? So run, that ye may obtain." [1 Corinthians 9:24.]

Spiritual discipline is important to cultivate for making personal and spiritual progress.
List the ways you'd like to develop spiritual discipline with prayer and meditation.

My thoughts:

_____

_____

_____

_____

OCTOBER
DAY 28

A man had a son with a mute spirit and brought him to the disciples—who couldn't address the situation. The problem was, the disciples had issues of disbelief; and as well, of the Father. Jesus called them out: "O faithless generation, how long shall I be with you?" Jesus told them to bring the boy to Him. He said to the man, "If you can believe, all things are possible to him that believe." The man cried out: "Lord, I believe." Jesus rebuked the unclean spirit and commanded it to come out and never to enter into the son again. The disciples asked Jesus: "Why could we not cast it out?" Jesus replied: "This kind does not go out except by prayer and fasting." [Matthew 17:17-21] If we're going to see breakthroughs in our region and neighborhoods, they'll only happen if we pray intensely and fast first.

*Developing spiritual discipline strengthens our faith.
Consider memorizing and repeating soulfully: "If you can
believe, all things are possible" to strengthen your resolve in
Christ and in serving Him.*

My thoughts:

_____

_____

_____

_____

OCTOBER
DAY 29

We must deal with areas in our lives that may face disbelief. When Jesus dealt with his disciples, He had to constantly deal with their disbeliefs. He called them a "faithless and perverse generation." [Matthew 17:17] We still find today that unbelief is at an all time high in the church. Jesus told the disciples to overcome unbelief with prayer and fasting. We, too,to must work through our unbeliefs to more properly experience the astounding blessings God wants to release in our lives. If you've faith as a mustard seed, nothing will be impossible for you!

Seed your pearls of faith and implicit belief in the word of the Lord.
How did your faith save you in a challenging situation?
What other situations tested your faith? How did you overcome them?

My thoughts:

_____

_____

_____

_____

OCTOBER
DAY 30

The power of prayer should not be underestimated. "The prayer of a righteous man is powerful and effective." [James 5:16-18] Elijah was a man just like us. He prayed earnestly that it would not rain, and it did not rain on the land for three and a half years. Again he prayed, and the heavens gave rain, and the earth produced its crops. God most definitely listens to our prayers, answers prayers and moves in response to our prayers. Jesus taught, "I tell you the truth, if you have faith as small as a mustard seed, you can say to this mountain, 'Move from here to there' and it will move. Nothing will be impossible for you." [Matthew 17:20] "The weapons we fight with are not the weapons of the world. On the contrary, they have divine power to demolish strongholds. We demolish arguments and every pretension that sets itself up against the knowledge of God, and we take captive every thought to make it obedient to Christ." [2 Corinthians 10:4-5] The Bible urges, "And pray in the Spirit on all occasions with all kinds of prayers and requests. With this in mind, be alert and always keep on praying for all the saints." [Ephesians 6:18] Devote yourself to the power of prayer!

Sincere prayerful efforts are always rewarded by God.
Get started and stay committed to daily prayer to guide and protect you.
Only, don't expect results according to human desires and expectations.

My thoughts:

_____

_____

_____

_____

OCTOBER
DAY 31

Establish a vision and create a strategic plan to position yourself to attract the spiritual resources neccesary to obtain spiritual growth. "But flee from these things, you man of God, and pursue righteousness, godliness, faith, love, perseverance and gentleness." [1 Timothy 6:11] The things that Paul says we should flee from are things that cause us to fall into temptation and ultimately bring destruction to our lives. The goal of spiritual growth and development is to become like Christ. Our every move should get us closer to this heavenly goal. "Fight the good fight of faith, lay hold on eternal life, whereunto thou art also called, and hast professed a good profession before many witnesses." [1 Timothy 6:12]

With the year ending soon, what's your vision to end this year with, on a positive note?
How will you develop your strategy (or plan) to achieve your goals?

My thoughts:
_____
_____
_____
_____

NOVEMBER
DAY 1

Ask God to give you your edge back in every area of your spiritual life and that you'll become even more fervent in spirit and for all things. The enemy of our souls wants us to give up and throw in the towel. But no matter how dificult life may be at this present time, recognize that quiting is not an option for those who have their hope in Christ Jesus. Bind the spirit of quiting and giving up in this season. Set loose the spirit of Jesus who urges us to be like Him. And let us not grow weary while doing good, for in due season we shall reap if we do not lose heart. [Galatians 6:9] At all times, keep this conviction at the forefront of your Kingdom consciousness: "I can do all things through Christ who strengthens me." [Philippians 4:13]

Walking in His grace means absolute consecration in giving our lives over to manifesting God.
It's not human submission to another power-hungry person, but a deeper commitment to the Real God Power in us when we're fervent in His spirit.
Your sincere cries to get your edge back will be heard—to do better for Him.

My thoughts:

_____

_____

_____

_____

NOVEMBER
DAY 2

When you need guidance, prayer and fasting can produce amazing Kingdom results. King Jehoshaphat (who was a godly leader) called the nation of Judah to fast and prayer after fighting the vast army consisting of Moabites, Ammonites and others. [2 Chronicles 20:3-4] As they sought the Lord with fasting, rather than running for their lives, they were frantic for God's direction and help. God responded by guiding them with His supernatural power. "You will not need to fight in this battle. Position yourselves, stand still and see the salvation of the Lord, who is with you, O Judah and Jerusalem! Do not fear or be dismayed; tomorrow go out against them, for the Lord is with you." [2 Chronicles 20:17]

The wealth of unwavering belief in God saves us time and again. At every moment, when we consecrate our thoughts and actions to Him, we reap relevant results—but only if we remember to consult His guidance.

My thoughts:

_____

_____

_____

_____

NOVEMBER
DAY 3

This is the day that the Lord will increase your levels of faith and release His divine healing and health unto you. As you intercede for your families, city and region, you'll see the Lord manifest Himself unto you and the things that you petition Him for. "For I know that this will turn out for my deliverance through your prayers and the provision of the Spirit of Jesus Christ." Philippians 1:19

What are some personal issues you're working through for yourself and family members?
What are those that you're running away from?
List them down and offer your petitions to Him for His salvation and divine satisfaction.

My thoughts:

_____

_____

_____

_____

NOVEMBER
DAY 4

Scripture states every believer has spiritual weapons they're able to use to defeat the enemy. These spiritual weapons of mass destruction are ordained by the Lord, unlike human-made weapons of mass destruction. Paul said, "For the weapons of our warfare are not carnal, but mighty in God for the pulling down of strongholds." [2 Corinthians 10:4] Paul wrote this letter to tell the Church they were engaged in a holy warfare. Warfare means conflict or battle; he was saying that each and every day we wake up, we engage in conflicts with the enemy of our souls—the devil. But, we have spiritual weapons given by God to fight with. The sporting and military worlds know you must be aware of who your enemy is. Paul said, "We wrestle not against flesh and blood, but against principalities, against powers, against the rulers of the darkness of this age, against spiritual host of wickedness in heavenly places." [Ephesians 6:12] Our fight is not against people, or flesh and blood, but against a host of demons within us that aim to defile, destroy, harass, tempt and enslave all humankind in wickedly unnatural ways.

The weapons of mass destruction are already inside us—battling us from the moment we wake, throughout the day and to the end of every day.
These unwholesome forces of darkness and destruction are ready to pounce anytime.
That's why we must invoke the higher powers of fortitude, willpower and determination to fight and exterminate them, by using our God-given higher spiritual weapons.

My thoughts:

_____

_____

_____

_____

NOVEMBER
DAY 5

Many of us have experienced breakthroughs or miracles this year. This testifies to our faithfulness in God when we hang in there and persevere. Continue to remain steadfast and immovable, in knowing that our labor and efforts will not be in vain. In struggling and adjusting to the day's demands and conflicts, make up your mind to be determined that *you can do it*! Hold your ground, do not be defeated! Today, pray against the "spirit of apathy" that causes us to be slothful, lazy, apprehensive, non-committed and lackadaisical in all things godly. Pray to get back your edge, spiritually and naturally. Also pray for breakthroughs in finances, health, employment and everything else going on in your lives!

Never quit! Spiritually and in all areas of life!
It's easy to develop bad habits of apathy, but hard to start good habits that benefit us.
What forces of apathy are holding you back? What will you do to overcome them?

My thoughts:

_____
_____
_____
_____

NOVEMBER
DAY 6

James said, "Therefore submit to God. Resist the devil and he will flee from you." [James 4"7] Recognize that the enemy is highly organized when he sends Spanky and the Gang after you. They're similar in getting orders from their commander-in-chief, Satan. And they carry them out to the "T!" But don't get discouraged. The word says, "That no weapon formed against us shall prosper." [Isaiah 54:17] Though Satan and his imps have some lesser power, the authority God has given us is totally far greater! "And these signs shall follow them that believe: In My Name shall they cast out devils." [Mark 16:17] Incredibly, God puts us in situations to battle against the enemy, no matter how the enemy attacks. So, wisely use your spiritual weapons of mass destruction to defeat them. What are some weapons to employ to experience the victory of God? Kingdom people use: fasting, invoking the Name of Jesus, the power of the Holy Spirit and His gifts, your sterling testimony, the blood, prayer, the word, and praise, to name a few. These are all spiritual weapons of mass destruction.

When was the first time you felt attacked by the hostile forces?
What spiritual weapons did you employ to fight them off?
What other spiritual weapons have you used since then?

My thoughts:

_____

_____

_____

_____

NOVEMBER
DAY 7

Everyone struggles through life, on life's battlefield. Take a moment this evening to call another brother or sister in Christ. Call them for encouragement and friendship. Take time to wrap your mind around how fasting helps purify your body, mind and overall consciousness. Launch out tomorrow morning in submitting to a fast. Fasting is not a hardship. You're foregoing one, two or three two meals a day—which is a sacrifice of purification unto God. This sacrifice sets you up for greater in God's work and glory. The Bible states that we can do all things through Christ who strengthens us. [Philippians 4:13]

Empower yourself through the power of fasting (which only means missing one, two or three meals a day).
Fasting is a cleansing and purifying ritual for body, spirit and overall consciousness.

My thoughts:

_____

_____

_____

_____

NOVEMBER
DAY 8

The Glory of God is the fullness of God. The fullness of God is His character and His attributes. We receive God's fullness by accepting Jesus Christ into our lives, Whom The Father has already glorified. "And now, O Father, glorify me together with yourself, with the glory which I had with you before the world was." [John 17:5] Jesus is crying out to The Lord, "Glorify me with you," by asking The Lord to bring Him into oneness and union with a closer, more intimate relationship. Jesus said: "I and my father are one." [John 10:30] Jesus wants us to experience the love of The Father, too. He wants us to experience this same bond and richness with The Father that He feels. Beloved, let us love one another, for love is of God and everyone who loves is born of God and knows God. [1 John 4:7]

Russian novelist Leo Tolstoy wrote a Christmas story on, "Where love is, God is."
God's very nature is loving oneness, a glorious all-embracing wealth of loving everyone by sharing; and as Christ wants to share with us, too.

My thoughts:
_____
_____
_____
_____

NOVEMBER
DAY 9

We believe in God not only to get our edge back, but also to heal from a spirit of apathy. Everyone has the ability to finish strongly our first week of consecration. Those who are fasting are depending on you and others to be prayerful and consecrated to more properly experience God. In our collective efforts, we're united in drawing closer and nearer unto Him, as we address the weak areas of our lives and offer our beliefs to God to transform in our region. Invite someone to join you to fast, who's outside of your own church family, so they may also experience the more profound breakthrough power of God. "But this kind does not go out except by prayer and fasting." [Matthew 17:21]

We're all empowered when we walk in the collective spirit of God.
No person is an island. We need each other to enrich our lives.
We spiritually enrich our lives by inviting and encouraging other people to fast and walk with us.

My thoughts:

_____

_____

_____

_____

NOVEMBER
DAY 10

"To everything there is a season, A time for every purpose under heaven: A time to be born, and a time to die, A time to plant, and a time to pluck what has been planted." [Ecclesiastes 3:1,2] It's very clear God moves in seasons. As well, scripture is clear God is in total control of everything that occurs. We must know the times and seasons of our lives to make the right spiritual decisions about our everyday lives and situations. For example, Zacharias and Elizabeth had been barren and arrived at old age. [Luke Chapter 1] In Old and New Testament times, when a woman was unable to bear children, she was frowned upon as someone smitten by God. But if with child, God shone His favor upon her. From a Biblical perspective, God never said anything of this nature; but man thought he knew the mind of God! Inadvertently, this became the thought as well as gospel. Moving into the New Testament, God needed to break through the false fables and myths made up by man—so people would renew their faith, and return to the true ways of the Lord.

Many are the false impressions people have fabricated about gospel and its practices.
Whenever in doubt, tell your concerns to an Elder and ask for clarification.
Never let misunderstandings cloud your thinking and living in truth.

My thoughts:

_____

_____

_____

_____

NOVEMBER
DAY 11

The disciples of Jesus couldn't rid a boy of a demon that caused him to fall into fire and into water. When Jesus commanded the demon to leave, and it did, the disciples asked Him why this demon didn't respond to them, as other demons had in the past. His answer: "Because of your unbelief; for assuredly, I say to you, if you have faith as a mustard seed, you will say to this mountain, 'Move from here to there,' and it will move; and nothing will be impossible for you." [Matthew 17:20,21] We're all in need of powerful acts in our lives to move mountains. If you've prayed, and prayed, and prayed, but still no results seem to appear, don't give up. Instead, make a bold move to do something you've not done before—and selflessly consecrate your actions to Him.

Sterling faith in our prayers to God moves mountains.
When was the last time you prayed hard, but didn't see
immediate results?
Did anything happen weeks, months, even years later—when you
were blessed with an awareness of how your prayer was
answered?

My thoughts:

_____

_____

_____

_____

NOVEMBER
DAY 12

Jesus said, "I am the way, the Truth, and the Life." God began the process of human transformation even before His Son, Jesus Christ, was born. Zacharias was a leader. He and his wife experienced great pain because of their difficulties in not having children. As a priest, Zacharias was responsible for serving in the temple along with fellow priests twice a year. This posed a problem for him and his wife due to the stigma that was placed upon them because they could not produce children and ultimately should have divorced. Once a year, they were to light the incense, which was a special event because it only happened every few years. Zacharias and his wife persevered through the silent and public criticisms and prayed to God whom they believed for a supernatural breakthrough instead of opting out of their assignment. Ultimately, they became the parents of John the Baptist. "And they were both righteous before God, walking in all the commandments and ordinances of the Lord blameless." [Luke 1:6] Be righteous to walk in the way of the Lord and keep on sustaining the ordinances Christ left for the church.

Living a righteous life is simple and natural.
Simply follow Christ and the ordinances He left behind.

My thoughts:
_____
_____
_____
_____

NOVEMBER
DAY 13

As we intercede on behalf of others, the Book of Mark recounts when the disciples were unable to help a man because they had not prepared with proper fasting and prayer. However, Jesus (who had completed a forty-day fast) was able to rebuke the foul spirit that plagued the man. When Jesus saw the people come running together, He rebuked the unclean spirit: "Deaf and dumb spirit, I command you, come out of him and enter him no more!" Then the unwholesome spirit cried out, convulsed and came out of the man. The man appeared dead. Many announced: "He is dead." But Jesus took him by the hand and lifted him up, and he arose. His disciples asked Him privately, "Why could we not cast it out?" He said, "This kind can come out by nothing but prayer and fasting." [Mark 9:25-29] This is significant and central to our intercession for others—with a deep, abiding faith.

What was the most significant spiritual intercession you did for a family member or friend?
What happened?
How did he or she recover, to become even stronger in their belief and gratitude to God?

My thoughts:

_____

_____

_____

_____

NOVEMBER
DAY 14

Let us press on today, in our prayer time with Him and to continue praying according to His will. With our undying faith, He'll save the lost in our city, region, across the country and as well, globally. We believe in God for an increase in His anointing and blessing us with the capacity to break every yoke and to lift every burden. Let us also be prayerful for the spirit of wisdom and revelation in knowing Him deeper, to better apply His guidance in our actions. Ultimately, we will come to know the exceeding greatness of His power towards us, for all who implicitly believe in Him.

Pray for "Thy Will Be Done" and end every prayer for His intercession to guide your actions.
There's no greater prayer than this simple, golden truth to manifest Him according to His Will.

My thoughts:

_____

_____

_____

_____

NOVEMBER
DAY 15

Fasting is an exercise that heals and empowers our spirit. It makes our spirit stronger, and our flesh weaker. As a result, we're more readily able to surrender to the Holy Spirit. Paul said: "I say then: Walk in the Spirit, and you shall not fulfill the lust of the flesh." [Galatians 5:16] The surrender of our individual will to His Perfect Will allows us to maintain our Christian walk. Fasting helps us stay focused on the path towards God's ordained destiny for our lives. The process of surrendering our individual will to His Will and allowing Him to govern our lives is activated more readily and abundantly through prayer, praise, worship and fasting.

Prayer, praise, worship and fasting are important to arrive at divine surrender unto His Will.
Divine surrender to God's will is totally different from human submission to another person.

My thoughts:

_____

_____

_____

_____

NOVEMBER
DAY 16

Fasting with the right motives puts us in a place of humility, which is a good place to be. Humility puts us in a place where we can receive more abundantly of God's grace. But God gives more than grace. He says: "God resists the proud, but gives grace to the humble." Therefore, submit to God." [James 4:6-7] Pride pushes us out of the presence of God. At the core of biblical fasting is that we humble ourselves before God and seek to discover and walk in His Will. David said, "I humbled myself with fasting." [Psalm 35:13] Ezra said, "I proclaimed a fast there at the river of Ahava, that we might humble ourselves before our God, to seek from Him the right way for us and our little ones and all our possessions." [Ezra 8:22]. In fasting, we come to realize and acknowledge that just as we're dependent on food for the body to survive, so are we utterly dependent upon God for every aspect of our lives. Let us humble ourselves under the Almighty hand of God.

Humility is a powerful weapon to put us in good places, to joyfully receive divine gifts.
Humble submission to God's Will shows how very dependent we are upon His grace unfolding in our lives, at every moment.
Offer gratitude and humility to praise and invoke God, ceaselessly.

My thoughts:

_____
_____
_____
_____

NOVEMBER
DAY 17

There are three things to do to experience God's season of blessing and supernatural intervention. First, we selflessly serve against all opposition, even though in our constant serving we may be misunderstood by family and friends. Second, P.U.S.H or "Pray Until Something Happens." Never stop believing in God, have child-like faith, however barren a situation may appear. Third, walk by faith and not fear. "For God did not give them the spirit of fear, but of love, and of power and of a sound mind." [2 Timothy 1:7] Fear causes us to be timid or apprehensive about our season and the promises of God. No matter what blows your way in life, know that God has a season when he'll show up and show you the way out. Paul said, "Grow not weary while doing good for in due season we shall reap if we do not lose heart." [Galatians 6:9] Walk with love and not fear, for this is your due season!

We need to emphasize more love than fear in our hearts, beliefs and actions.
What are some positive and encouraging acts of love you've engaged in lately?
Again, love is not carnal lust—but heartfelt caring, concern and affection that we offer unconditionally to people, pets, plants, special and daily events; even our cars.

My thoughts:

_____

_____

_____

_____

NOVEMBER
DAY 18

John prayed and commended Gaius: "Prosper in all things, and be in health, as his soul prospered." [3 John 2] Gaius had been extremely hospitable and charitable in helping build up the ministry. Realize that this is a spiritual journey we're all on, in and with the Lord. On this journey, we have a responsibility to ensure our spiritual condition is in top shape. Being spiritually fit includes: physical, material and emotional wellbeing. The simple secret to spiritual fitness is: be sound in our faith. David said, "Blessed is the man that walks not in the counsel of the ungodly, nor stands in the path of sinners, nor sits in the seat of the scornful." [Psalm 1:1] Hold fast to the Truth "for the Truth will set us free" in Christ Jesus. We must be hospitable and charitable to our brethren and strangers. Give to those who are in need and support those of the faith as they minister unto us. Charity is important for believers to offer of themselves and their substance—unconditionally. We love all people and care for them when called upon. Paul said, "For the love of God compels us to do our very best to meet any need. These qualities enable us to be spiritually fit to do Kingdom business and to occupy until He comes." [2 Corinthian. 5:14]

How spiritually fit do you feel today?
What are unconditional and charitable giving you're most proud of having done?
List them; periodically refer to them to reinforce your ongoing good works to stay spiritually fit.

My thoughts:

_____

_____

_____

_____

NOVEMBER
DAY 19

But the fruit of the Spirit is: love, joy, peace, long-suffering, kindness, goodness, faithfulness, gentleness and self-control. Precious graces develop in a believer when the Holy Spirit fully controls his life. The first deals with our attitude towards God, in our love for Him. "A new commandment I give to you that you love one another; as I have loved you. By this all know that you are my disciples, if you have love for one another." [John 13:34] The second deals with our social relationships: "And be kind to one another, tenderhearted, forgiving one another, even as God in Christ forgave you." [Ephesians 4:32] The third deals with our Christian conduct. "See then that you walk circumspectly, not as fools but as wise, redeeming the time, because the days are evil. Therefore do not be unwise, but understand what the will of the Lord is." [Ephesians 5:15-17]

Divine love is the real deal.
Love God, see God in everyone and walk with wisdom in Christ.

My thoughts:
_____
_____
_____
_____

NOVEMBER
DAY 20

As we fast unto the Lord, we feel an excitement in gaining victory over the enemy. It's perhaps similar to when the children of Israel were at war with the tribes of Benjamin (who were opposing the spiritual move God had proclaimed for the Israelites). The children of Israel, being led by the Spirit, went up into the House of God. They wept, fasted and burned offerings, along with peace offerings, until evening. Their expressions of devotion to follow God's orders resulted in a glorious Israelite victory over the Benjamites. [Judges 20:25,26 & 28-48] Thank God for our victories! Continually praise God and live by His word for eternal victory.

Obedience to God shows good common sense to follow a sound spiritual discernment.
As human beings, we're not in full command of fighting for God's victory—but He is, and He will show the way to eternal victory if we but invoke His help at every step.

My thoughts:
_____
_____
_____
_____

NOVEMBER
DAY 21

The desire for food is basic to all living creatures. It's one of the strongest motivational forces at work in the body, even before birth. Babies are born with the natural instinct to reach out for their mother's breast. We can combine this intense natural desire with our natural spiritual desire for communion with our spiritual source to result in a greater intensity for the purposes of prayer and fasting. By combining our natural and spiritual desires, we summon the urgency of our petitions to come up before the throne of God. This intensity prompts Him to hear and answer us. "Delight thyself also in the Lord and He shall give thee the desires of thine heart." [Psalm 37:4] "What things soever ye desire, when ye pray, believe that ye receive them, and ye shall have them." [Mark 11:24] The stronger our desire, the more intensity we show in prayer, the more effective our prayers will become!

To desire physical nourishment is naturally human.
To desire God's nurturing is divinely elevating.
Combining both approaches with our intense prayers moves God
to respond, in His Way.

My thoughts:

_____

_____

_____

_____

NOVEMBER
DAY 22

Many are the afflictions of the righteous but the Lord delivers us out of them all. [Psalm 34:19] The hand of God is upon you and you are delivered from the hands of the enemy. [Ezra 8:31] We are not defeated. We are victorious in the Lord. Today we can rejoice knowing that we are on the side of the Lord. He has sent angels to fight on our behalf. So be encouraged as you go about this day knowing that the mighty hand of the Lord protects you.

God's protection is unconditional for those who believe in Him. Simply invoke divine protection before, during and after everything you do.

My thoughts:

_____

_____

_____

_____

NOVEMBER
DAY 23

Jesus chooses only those who are worthy to be in His army. He went after serious disciples. "Many are called, but few are chosen." [Matthew 22:14] Among the called and chosen, there's another category, those who are faithful. When God is looking for the best soldiers, He's looking for those who will answer His call. For those who would be saved, are filled with the Holy Ghost, full of the Word and above all—meet the requirement to be faithful. The Word of the Lord says: "Moreover it is required in stewards that one be found faithful." [1 Corinthians 4:2]

Our faith in Christ saves us at every moment.
As Kingdom citizens, our faith in Him is unwavering.

My thoughts:
_____
_____
_____
_____

NOVEMBER
DAY 24

There's no better time to give thanks unto the Lord than right now. What are you going through, that would not give you cause to pause and give God thanks? We thank Him because He is good, and because we put our trust and confidence in Him. We know that His grace will see us through any situation. "O give thanks unto the Lord; for he is good: because his mercy endureth forever." [Psalm 118:1] In the best of times, and even when situations are not so favorable, "It is a good thing to give thanks unto the Lord, and to sing praises unto thy name, O Most High." [Psalm 92:1]

God deserves our continuous and undying gratitude for all He does for us.
Gratitude to God is a surefire way to enter, and forever stay in, God's loving heart.

My thoughts:

_____

_____

_____

_____

NOVEMBER
DAY 25

There is an importance behind expressing gratitude to someone for the things that they do for you. It's like receiving a cool glass of water on a hot summer day. Just to know that someone appreciates the effort you took to do something special or make something happen in their life is priceless. Being thankful can also impact the quality of your own life, because it keeps you mindful of the blessings that you have. When you're thankful, you're less apt to complain about what you feel may be lacking in your life. Nothing will be able to hinder your praise. Apostle Paul helps us understand this in the Word of God: "In everything give thanks; for this is the will of God in Christ Jesus for you." [1 Thessalonians 5:18]

Offering gratitude is priceless to help us better appreciate our blessings.
It costs nothing to offer a heartfelt "thank you," while elevating everyone's consciousness.

My thoughts:

_____

_____

_____

_____

NOVEMBER
DAY 26

God's presence, power and unlimited resources are available to us in the name of Jesus Christ. Yet Jesus' name isn't a magic word to use to get what we want. In truth, we must pray according to God's Will, which we find in His Word. Jesus said: "If you remain in Me and My words remain in you, ask whatever you wish, and it will be given you." [John 15:7] The backbone of prayer is our total agreement with, and obedience to, God's Word, our oneness with Christ, who is the Living Word and our unity with God's purposes and His Will. Power in prayer is not based on human emotions, feelings or theories of men, but upon the Word of God, "which lives and abides forever." [1 Peter 1:23] His Word is the guarantee to answer our prayers, in His Own Way.

Pray unconditionally for His Will Be Done.
The intensity and sincerity of our cries are always heard by Him.
God responds in His Own Way according to the needs of each individual.

My thoughts:

_____

_____

_____

_____

NOVEMBER
DAY 27

Why not come to the place in your heart where you can say, "Lord, I forgive everybody of everything?" We can then let go of our claims for justice and repayment. The injustices are laid to rest at the cross, and the mercy and grace of Christ will flow into our lives. Love is the real power that purifies a multitude of sins. [1 Peter 4:8] The Kingdom of God is not about keeping religious rules, regulations and rituals; it's about righteousness, peace and joy in the Holy Spirit. All of which pleases God and even receives human approval. Precious joy blesses us when we live and remain in the rightful place of heartfelt mercy and forgiveness.

Live in joyful forgiveness.
This Thanksgiving season and onwards, aim to live in heartfelt peace and joy.
Your peaceful and joyful consciousness will impact and influence others positively.

My thoughts:

_____

_____

_____

_____

NOVEMBER
DAY 28

Let us have the mind of Christ. What is the mind of Christ, that we should also strive to have? Is it unconditional love, unmerited favor upon all who choose to follow Him? Is it infinite levels of forgiveness? God gives so many precious gifts that we should not take them all for granted. Just like He gives to us, we should also share them with others. Every good gift and every perfect gift is from above. [James 1:17]

It's sometimes hard to show love and mercy, especially when we're caught up in the hustle and bustle of life.
It's perhaps easier as Kingdom citizens when we consciously try to maintain the gold standard of showing love, mercy and honesty.

My thoughts:

_____

_____

_____

_____

NOVEMBER
DAY 29

God is prophetically taking us to the threshing floor. The Lord is breaking off that hard outer shell or husk and preparing us to become food for sustaining nations and this region. When grain is separated from chaff, wheat is ready for use. People asked John the Baptist if he was the Messiah. He answered them, "I baptize you with water. But One more powerful than I will come, the thongs of Whose sandals I am not worthy to untie. He will baptize you with the Holy Spirit and with fire." [Luke 3:16] We love these familiar verses and have heard many messages on receiving the Holy Spirit. But let's read the words that follow: "His winnowing fork is in His hand to clear His threshing floor and to gather the wheat into His barn, but He will burn up the chaff with unquenchable fire." [Luke 3:17] The Lord is telling us that He's committed to burning up the chaff in our lives. This is central to our relationship with Him. The Lord wants to knock the chaff off to set us free, to burn away undesirable things so we will, with a pure heart, flow in the grace, love and mercy of God.

God's grace is always there for our taking. We only have to ask. And we have to be pure in heart to receive His love and mercy. What qualities would you like to offer up as chaff, to discard forever?

My thoughts:

_____

_____

_____

_____

NOVEMBER
DAY 30

"And they that shall be of thee shall build the old waste places: thou shalt raise up the foundations of many generations; and thou shalt be called, The repairer of the breach, The restorer of paths to dwell in." [Isaiah 58:12] As believers we show kindness, charity, justice and generosity to everyone. God has strategically placed each of us in places where we can release godly characteristics onto the earthly realm. As you relate to different people coming cross your path today, be sensitive and receptive to the spirit of God guiding you. Consciously heed yourselves to the move of God, no matter what your flesh and desires may say otherwise—to avoid detouring to a less desirable day of unfruitful offerings.

Showing kindness and compassion to others is like selflessly offering First Fruit.
The spirit of God in people's hearts will respond to our love offerings and oneness.
And as amazing, trigger more positive feelings to emerge in yet other people they'll meet along their day's journey.

My thoughts:

_____

_____

_____

_____

DECEMBER
DAY 1

God's river of refreshment is designed for the stumbling. Those who are stable are sustained for a time by their own agility, but the stumbling man is desperate for his divine refreshment. The Bible says, "He gives power to the weak, And to those who have no might He increases strength. Even the youths shall faint and be weary, And the young men shall utterly fall, But those who wait on the Lord Shall renew their strength; They shall mount up with wings like eagles, They shall run and not be weary, They shall walk and not faint" [Isaiah 40:29-31] We'll always fail if we don't return to God; to look only to Him for support! In the words of the hymnist, we "Dare not trust the sweetest frame, but wholly lean on Jesus name!" May God's peace always guard and guide your heart and mind in Christ Jesus!

Everyone stumbles every now and again, while traveling along life's highway.
But we must learn to pick up our weary selves and not give up.
We'll always be refreshed by Christ's power by turning to Him—it's that simple!

My thoughts:

_____

_____

_____

_____

DECEMBER
DAY 2

To some of you, the word rest may be foreign or something that doesn't enter your vocabulary very often. But take the time to slow down during this season and, yes, rest. The year is well spent. You've done well on your job, with your family and church responsibilities. God is giving you permission to put the cell phone away, turn off the computer, not respond to an email, take a seat and just rest. Rest is waiting for you. "There remaineth therefore a rest to the people of God." [Hebrews 4:9] God provides a quiet time for rest and relaxation. The work is done. He finished it at Calvary when He hung as a curse on the tree for our salvation. Christ redeemed us from the curse of the law, having become a curse for us; for it is written, "Cursed is everyone who hangs on a tree." [Galatians 3:13] Even though Mary and Martha both had the responsibility of cooking and cleaning for the general wellbeing of, and hospitality for, Jesus, guests and disciples that frequented their home, Mary used the opportunity to lay at the feet of Jesus, where she could receive rest.

Our physical bodies need to rebalance, to spend quiet time at the feet of the Lord.
Being at His feet means taking time to rest up and rejuvenate with peaceful meditation, quiet joy and gratitude—in allowing His Peace to refresh and reenergize us for the New Year's work.

My thoughts:

_____

_____

_____

_____

DECEMBER
DAY 3

Zumba® is a high intensity workout that involves dance and aerobic elements to move you into good health and fitness. The principal behind Zumba® is to get fit while having fun. It all started in Colombia in the nineties when aerobics teacher Beto Perez forgot his usual music and had to improvise around the music he had in his car, which was traditional Latin salsa and merengue. Since then, millions around the world have joined the Zumba® craze. After trying it, I've found that the best part is in the cooling down, after an hour of high-energy working out. God wants us to be fit and work out spiritually, physically and mentally. Yet, when we have exerted all we can, we must not forget to take time to cool down. As the disciples were preparing to partake of the Last Supper with our Lord and Savior, the disciple whom He loved, laid on His bosom. [John 13:23] Not only do we cool down to rest up from what has already occurred, but also in anticipation of what is to come.

Cooling off is quiet time well spent, to wind down and gradually return to room consciousness.
When we cool down, we're in a more reflective and meditative mood to better assimilate the positive effects of staying fit—and ready for the next move.

My thoughts:

_____

_____

_____

_____

DECEMBER
DAY 4

Adaptability and flexibility go hand in hand. That's because being adaptable is being flexible in going with the flow when things change. Because the world is ever changing, other things in our lives are bound to change, too. Such as changes in: the economy, our families and in the environment. We're transitioning from one season to another season. Some may be literally moving from one location in the neighborhood or to another city, state or country. Whatever situation we find ourselves in now, we shouldn't get too comfortable—especially when we know that God is in control. We have to be willing to adopt a flexible approach to the manner in which we live our lives. What is God's plan for our lives? During our period of predestination, how was success defined for us before we were born? God declares that His thoughts are not our thoughts and His ways are not our ways. [Isaiah 55:8] Let us remain confident as well, that He means us good (not evil or stumbling) with every step that He orders for us. Our prayer is to be willing to accept God's plans for our lives and to get into agreement with every thought, in adapting to the Holy Spirit, because He is God.

Stay flexible and focused on God's plan for your life.
Often, our human demands and unspiritual expectations make it hard to hear God's word.
Being flexible, adjustable and adaptable will help us go with divine flow to realize God's plan.

My thoughts:

_____

_____

_____

_____

DECEMBER
DAY 5

What is that fragrance that you have on today? The aroma of the anointing smells good on you. Have you ever been asked about the type of perfume or cologne you're wearing? That seems a simple enough question, that I'm sure if asked, you'd be happy to share the answer. But have you ever thought that the smell they were actually experiencing wasn't the smell of a body splash or spray—but the aroma of the Holy Spirit that dwells inside you? The smell of every true, born-again believer is the aroma of the Holy Spirit. "Because of the fragrance of your good ointments, Your name *is* ointment poured forth." [Song of Solomon 1:3] The anointing isn't too bold or overpowering, but just right to provide a hint of joy, love and peace to your soul. It lets those who are seeking God know that you are a child of His.

Do you love and appreciate the sweet smell and breath of babies?
Babies are pure and innocent in sporting the scent of God in their little bodies.
We recapture the sweet essence of our souls when we breathe life back into our spiritual seeking with prayer and meditation—and are re-anointed with the fragrance of the Holy Spirit.

My thoughts:

_____

_____

_____

_____

DECEMBER
DAY 6

The Holy Spirit is alive and well and is represented in the Bible in the form of a person rather than a thing. Who is the Holy Spirit and why is His work important to the believer? The Holy Spirit is God and the third part of the Holy Trinity, The Father and Son, being the first two. He has intellect, passions and will and can be grieved according to the Word of God. [Ephesians 4:30] The Spirit is always at work, ultimately leading us all toward Christ. He can act in any way He needs to do what needs to be done, in leading us into a better relationship with the Lord. The Holy Spirit can speak, testify, appoint, lead and shape the life of any person. Since He can do all of these and more, we need not get in the way. The Holy Spirit lives within each of us and knows just what we need, to do God's work. Do you not know that your bodies are temples of the Holy Spirit residing in you, whom you have received from God? For those who are led by the Spirit of God are the children of God. [Romans 8:14]

You are not your own thoughts or inclinations of mind and ego. When you shift your focus and reliance from the doubting mind to the loving heart, your confidence will have a chance to shine forth the Holy Spirit—as a true child of God.

My thoughts:

_____

_____

_____

_____

DECEMBER
DAY 7

A deeper relationship with God begins with conscious action and determination on our part. "But take diligent heed, to love the Lord your God, and to walk in all His ways, and to keep His commandments, and to cleave unto Him, and to serve Him with all of your heart and soul." [Joshua 22:5] "Draw near to God, and He will draw near to you." [James 4:8] Five practices help draw us nearer to God:

1. Love. "Thy shall love the Lord your god, with all of your heart, and with the soul, and with your might." [Deuteronomy 6:5]

2. Walk in Him. "He that saith he abideth in Him ought himself also so to walk, even as He walked." [1 John 2:6]

3. Keep the faith. "For this is the love of God, that we keep His commandments; and His commandments are not grievous." [1 John 5:3]

4. Cleave and stay in Him. "Therefore, my beloved brethren, be ye steadfast, unmovable, always abounding in the work of the Lord, for as much as ye know that your labour is not in vain in the Lord." [1 Corinthians 15:58]

5. Serve selflessly. "Not with eye service as men pleasers, but as the servants of Christ, doing the will of God from the heart. With good will doing service, as to the Lord, and not to men: knowing that whatsoever good thing any man doeth, the same shall he receive of the Lord, whether he be bond or free." [Ephesians. 6:6-8]

Our conscious and determined actions forge a deeper, closer relationship with God.
His unconditional Love is our eternal salvation when we keep our walk in Him.

My thoughts:

_____

_____

_____

_____

DECEMBER
DAY 8

If we are going to be victorious, God has to fight the battle in and through us. But we also have to be divinely armed. "Do not fear or be dismayed because of this great multitude, for the battle is not yours but God's." [2 Chronicles 20:15] Antoinette's faith was tested in 2013 when twenty-year-old Michael Hill walked into the Ronald E. McNair Learning Academy in Decatur, Georgia. Michael was armed with an AK-47, five hundred rounds of ammunition and in his words, "Nothing to live for." Antoinette's deep-seated faith proved victorious when she spent nearly fourteen minutes sharing the love of God with this mentally disturbed individual. She shared her own pain, which brought him into a more uplifting relationship with her. Even in our own pain, we can help others out of theirs. She clearly put God on the front line and God cleared the path for success for her and the hundreds of children that could have been affected by Michael's behavior. Through her faith in God, Antoinette was able to show genuine love to the perpetrator that he came to surrender. Have faith in God, and faith that He saves us all, all the time.

Be aware of, and thankful to, God for His guidance with your every thought and action.
This is the saving grace of having implicit faith, in proclaiming His word at every moment.
Antoinette's oneness with Michael's problem shows how the Holy Spirit works in and through us, to proclaim God's eternal victory in everyone.

My thoughts:

_____

_____

_____

_____

DECEMBER
DAY 9

Dealing with a tragedy or failed circumstance in your life can be difficult to handle. When you cry out to God during these times, He will always be available to help you. God is the constant friend who will be with you through every difficult issue or situation that you encounter. Choose to praise God when things are going well and continue to praise Him even if things are not. Many scriptures demonstrate God as our helper in times of trouble. "For in the time of trouble He shall hide me in His pavilion: in the secret of His tabernacle shall He hide me; He shall set me up upon a rock." [Psalm 27:5] God will keep you safe until the storm passes over. He will revive, refresh and renew your spirit and soul. David cried, "No one cares for my soul. I cry to you, O Lord; I say, 'You are my refuge, my portion in the land of the living.' Attend to my cry, for I am brought very low! Deliver me from my persecutors, for they are too strong for me! Bring me out of prison that I may give thanks to your name! The righteous will surround me, for You will deal bountifully with me." [Psalm 142:4-7]

God is our eternal friend, forever and forever more.
While human friendships may fail over time, God is most
reassuringly there for us at our hour of need.

My thoughts:

_____

_____

_____

_____

December
Day 10

Just like with any mother who's very protective of her young, God is also very protective of us, His children. Children are very vulnerable and susceptible to misuse or abuse at the hands of anyone who would try to take advantage of them. The Lord takes it personally when someone sets out to harm a child of His and deals with them accordingly. "Your enemies have ridiculed, Lord, how they have ridiculed every step of Your anointed." [Psalm 89:51] But don't be unduly concerned, for their lives (and yours) are in the hands of the Lord. Even though people may have doubted your ability to finish strong this year, you have been made to triumph. Paul wrote, "Thanks be to God, who always leads us in His triumph in Christ, and manifests through us the sweet aroma of the knowledge of Him in every place." [2 Corinthians 2:14]

Our childlike sweetness is God's very own fragrance that
protects and saves us at every moment.
Our childlike innocence leads us triumphantly to manifest God's
sweet fragrance in everything we say and do.
Thus, your divine fragrance connects with those who are waiting
and receptive to be awakened, to welcome their own Holy Spirit.
Their souls will be grateful to you.

My thoughts:

_____

_____

_____

_____

DECEMBER
DAY 11

In Colossians 3:5-9, Paul shows us some of the results in setting our minds on Christ. We're able to put off old practices such as greed, anger and dishonesty because we've "laid aside the old self with it's evil practices, and have put on the new self." After working out or doing yard work, followed by showering, do you put back on your old, sweaty clothes? Although they were good enough to sweat in, why aren't they acceptable after showering? Because you've cleaned up. (However, if you forgot you took a shower, then the clothes you put back on may not matter that much.) But once you know you're clean, you want to dress properly to reflect your new condition. It's the same with your mind. Clean up your act. Once Jesus Christ has cleansed you with His blood, there's no need to go back to put on your old thought patterns. You've the mind of Christ as a believer now. You just need to develop the discipline of thinking with a Kingdom mind. Put on New Thoughts!

Cleanliness in mind and attitude is godliness, when we set our minds on Christ.
What new practices will you welcome as a believer?
What uncomely practices will you work on, to further clean up your act?

My thoughts:

_____

_____

_____

_____

DECEMBER
DAY 12

The Bible says: "That God would never leave us nor forsake us." [Hebrews 13:5] Thus the devil is a liar when he brings on you those kinds of thoughts. We all have somebody whom we call special in our lives, whom we enjoy spending time with, especially when we need a caring touch. They can be far or near, as none of us are friendless. Jesus is an eternal friend who sticks and binds closer than a brother, so don't allow the enemy to play with your mind and cause you to be in a rut this holiday season. David said: "Lift up your heads, O you gates! and be lifted up, you everlasting doors! And the King of Glory shall come in." [Psalm 24:7] Who is this King of Glory? The Lord strong and mighty, The Lord mighty in battle and in peaceful joy.

Friends are wonderful to uplift our spirits when we need cheering up.
But Christ is our forever friend who loves us and fights for us to eternity.

My thoughts:

_____

_____

_____

_____

DECEMBER
DAY 13

Don't believe the hype. All of us inevitably experience situations that are hyped out of control and out of proportion. The prince of darkness and uncomely influences of the world will attack each one of us in the areas of: lust of the flesh, in pride of life, or lust of the eyes. But thank God we have the sword of the spirit. This is our divine sword to back off the enemy with. Jesus was able to defeat him with the word; so can we. [Matthew 4:1-4] But we have to say it with authority and mean it as we persevere through the hype. Disavow the hype as it'll only cause you to abort the call that's on your life—which prevents you from accomplishing the plan that you *know* God has for you.

What does hype mean? Too good to be true!
Don't give in to temptations of the flesh, pride or any kind of vanity.
Declare outright you're for God with your God-blessed power and authority.

My thoughts:

_____
_____
_____
_____

DECEMBER
DAY 14

We have to be good soldiers in the service of Jesus. [2 Timothy 2:3] His battles are our battles that we're in for the duration of, every lifetime. Satan has declared war: it's either conquest or be conquered. But don't ever be afraid you won't fit in with the world. You're not supposed to fit in with the world of lost temptations. We have to be in the world—but not of the world that corrupts. We don't have to mix in with the world of lowly temptations. The world hungers for popularity and self-imposed importance. But refuse to let the world corrupt you. We are salt and light; the influencer, not the influenced. When the world can't tell you apart from lowly temptations, that means your light has gone out and your salt has lost it savor.

The world is a hotbed of unholy temptation and corruption such as self-imposed importance.
But don't be led astray by self-power and worldly influence that blinds us to real wealth—in adhering to oneness with God's Word.

My thoughts:

_____

_____

_____

_____

DECEMBER
DAY 15

Why go to church? A church-goer wrote a letter to the editor of a newspaper to complain that it made no sense to go to church every Sunday. "I've gone for 30 years now," he wrote, "and in that time I've heard about 3,000 sermons. But for the life of me, I can't remember a single one of them. So, I think I'm wasting my time and the pastors are wasting theirs by giving sermons." This started a real controversy in the *Letters to the Editor* column—much to the delight of the editor. It went on for weeks. Until someone wrote this clincher: "I've been married for 30 years now. In that time, my wife has cooked some 32,000 meals. But, for the life of me, I cannot recall the entire menu for a single one of those meals. But I do know this. They all nourished me and gave me the strength I needed to do my work. If my wife had not given me these meals, I would be physically dead today. Likewise, if I had not gone to church for holy nourishment, I would be spiritually dead today!" When you're DOWN to nothing, God is UP to something! Faith sees the invisible, believes the incredible and receives the impossible!

Even though your mind is incapable of seeing the reality of divinity, your heart's faith will nourish and uplift your spirit for eternity.
Take for real the invisible, enduring goodness of faith to raise you up every time you need it!

My thoughts:

_____

_____

_____

_____

DECEMBER
DAY 16

The Bible says, "The Kingdom of heaven is like a man who sowed good seed in his field." [Matthew 13:24] If we want a bountiful harvest, we must sow the seeds of self, of our substance and service. The farmer knows nothing can be harvested unless something worthy is sown. God walked in His own principle of sowing when He gave His only and begotten Son, and sowed Him into the earthly realm. Now, He's reaping from the seed that was sown. Hence, we're His harvest known as the church or body of believers. Sowing into good ground produces good fruit—and plenty of it, too. Align your thoughts and hearts with this simple principle: watch God show up and show out every season of your life!

When we intentionally sow good thoughts and acts, in season
and out, God is there to help us reap the rewards.
His joy and pride in us will be boundless.

My thoughts:

_____

_____

_____

_____

DECEMBER
DAY 17

Scripture tells us God has released His light in each of us so we would be illuminated for Him. God gave Isaiah a prophetic word for the Jews: "Arise, Shine, for they Light has come! And the Glory of the Lord is risen upon you." [Isaiah 60:1] This word transcends to our dispensation and speaks to us right where we are in this season of our lives. We may be frustrated, feeling rejected and depressed in this wintery time. When this occurs, we tend to take on vices that become dark secrets, thus causing us to slip even further away from being illuminated in Christ. And end up being taken advantage of by the devil. These unfruitful habits may seem to placate us for the moment, but will never last long enough to heal us. These habits are distractions that come with consequences that ultimately can be death threatening. Isaiah, the eagle-eyed prophet said: "Instead of laying down and giving up, Arise, stand up" to symbolize your recovery, deliverance and restoration. Face your opposition on your feet and flourish in a prosperous state, instead of letting the enemy get the best of you! Arise and Shine!

What bad habits are getting the better of you?
How will you work through these self-defeating habits to recover and restore your goodness and godliness?
What positive attributes would you like to start developing now—to be better prepared to excel and revel in your rewards for this coming year?

My thoughts:

_____

_____

_____

_____

DECEMBER
DAY 18

We must be about our Father's business if we're going to see and experience the astounding things that God will do in this next season of our lives. We must be "steadfast and unmovable," and committed to the divine call that's upon us. This year has brought great exponential growth into the lives of the people of God because He wants to flourish in us and fulfill His word in us. "Therefore, my beloved brethren, be ye steadfast, unmovable, always abounding in the work of the Lord, forasmuch as ye know that your labor is not in vain in the Lord." [1 Corinthians 15:58]

God's pride in us, His children of light, is boundless.
Therefore, take pride and joy in upholding His trust in us and
His limitless gifts for our growth and deliverance.
We will be satisfied divinely. So will God.

My thoughts:

_____

_____

_____

_____

DECEMBER
DAY 19

To be truly and fully successful, you must give back to those around you who are in need. If you want to reposition yourself for ongoing and sustained success, then please incorporate a generous and compassionate spirit in your equation in attending to their ministry and physical needs. However, also realize that the needs of this world are insatiable. "The horse leach hath two daughters, crying, give, give. There are three things that are never satisfied, yea, four things say not. It is enough: The grave; and the barren womb; the earth that is not filled with water; and the fire that saith not, It is enough." [Proverbs 30:14,15]

We've heard the saying, "give till it hurts." And that's good when our efforts yield positive results in helping others. However, also be wise in your hearts to know when enough is enough.

My thoughts:

_____

_____

_____

_____

DECEMBER
DAY 20

We've entered into the holiday season to celebrate the birth of our Lord and Savior, Jesus Christ. Over 2,000 years ago, God gave us His only and begotten Son so that we would have a right to the tree of life. This is the time to really put the emphasis on Him for all that He has done for us with His munificent gifts. As God gives generously, we should also be in the mode of giving selflessly of ourselves, our service and substance unto Him. Everyday God meets our needs and supplies us with seeds that can be sown again and again, so we always have the ability to be His sowers. We're created to be a blessing not only to ourselves, but also to others. This is a principle we must walk in as Christians, to continuously reap in every season. The Lord loves us; we show Him how much we love Him too, by keeping His commandments. God certainly loves it when we tell Him we love Him, but He loves it even more when we show Him through good works. Walk in that spirit as you prepare for Christmas. Be careful not to get caught up in the season's materialistic commerce. Make the Lord a top priority in your home and heart temples; watch God open the window of heaven's blessings to you. Don't be like the grinch who stole Christmas; be like the Wise Men who were givers.

It takes very little to give of ourselves. Volunteer wherever there's a need that also gives you joy.
Whether at home, church or soup kitchen, when we give selflessly, the deep satisfaction we get is our blessed reward.

My thoughts:

_____

_____

_____

_____

DECEMBER
DAY 21

As we celebrate the birth of Christ, pray to be blessed with the spirit of Mary when she said: "My soul magnifies the Lord, and my spirit has rejoiced in God my Savior." [Luke 1:46] To magnify the Lord means to declare the greatness of God. Let's rejoice in God for the great things He has done, and exalt His name. Through every personal storm and trial we experience every year, God has been great! We declare now and forever that it was nobody but God, Who met, and continues to meet, our every need.

In this sacred season celebrating the birth of Christ, look back on all His gifts to you.
What are you most thankful for?
What gifts of the spirit are you looking forward to receiving? List them and be inspired to open your heart even more to receive His boundless blessings!

My thoughts:

_____

_____

_____

_____

DECEMBER
DAY 22

David expressed a deep and loving desire to go to God. "As the deer pants for streams of water, so my soul pants for you, my God. My soul thirsts for God, for the living God. When can I go and meet with God?" [Psalm 42:1-2] He compared it to the desire of a deer whose thirst can only be quenched by a cool drink of water that flows freely from the brook. Similarly, the Lord is that revitalizing refreshment and gift of life for us, too. David is so encouraged by the anticipation of being able to meet with God, it's like a childlike infatuation in getting to Him, to be divinely nourished and nurtured. David thirsts and longs for the presence of God, desiring to be in communion and fellowship with God. How much do you love God?

How ardent is your divine desire to meet God?
Will you yearn for God as you yearn for gasps of air to stay alive?

My thoughts:

_____

_____

_____

_____

DECEMBER
DAY 23

"The Lord your God will raise up for you a prophet like me from among you, from your countrymen, you shall listen to him." [Deuteronomy 18:15] Are you waiting for your promotion or for a promised reward to be realized? If God said it, then you can believe wholeheartedly He'll do it. Don't listen to the naysayers as they try to make you feel as if you don't deserve the blessings and favors God is pouring down on you. And certainly don't listen to lies that Satan tells you because they'll only create strongholds in your mind, and strangle you by making it difficult to overcome false fears and doubts. Don't let anyone trick you out of what God has for you. [Colossians 2:18] You are worthy of your reward. Just hang in there through thick and thin.

It's all too easy to give in to naysayers who are jealous of your striving to be the best in God.
Be patient with yourself; endure false fears and taunts.
Stay the course and you'll be rewarded by the Lord.

My thoughts:

_____

_____

_____

_____

DECEMBER
DAY 24

In a world where everyone is trying to fit in and be accepted, this is a very important news flash. Children of God are not supposed to fit in with the world. People naturally want to be accepted by the crowd or be invited to the party. But don't be concerned about being left out. You've been chosen by God—which is far greater than the choice of the world. God has selected you and inducted you into a very exclusive and divine club. "We are a chosen people, a royal priesthood, a holy nation, a people belonging to God, that you may declare the praise of Him who called you out of darkness into His wonderful light." [1 Peter 2:9] Since we belong to God, God desires to have fellowship with us. He'll accept us and bring us before great men. God is calling you to get closer to Him today and at every moment!

Never ever feel left out of a party invitation or to be with a crowd of people.
Instead, rise to the occasion and offer thanks for His choice selection in admitting you to the highest club—to serve Him selflessly.

My thoughts:

_____

_____

_____

_____

DECEMBER
DAY 25

There was a time when man hid from the presence of God [Genesis 3:8] and a time afterwards because of sin. We were not able to look on the presence of God and live. [Exodus 33:20] But in the hustle and bustle of the Holiday season and during this time of family, sharing and gift giving, we need to take some time to be in the *presence* of God. It's in His presence that we find the gift of life and true joy. "You make known to me the path of life; in Your presence there is fullness of joy; at your right hand are pleasures forevermore." [Psalm 16:11] The psalmist describes a great joy when he realizes that the Lord will not leave him and that His presence sustains him. The reality is that God will never leave us nor will he forsake us. [Hebrews 13:5] God will not allow our spirit in man to be utterly destroyed, even though we may cause God to become angry due to our uncomely sins and disobedience. God's presence is always with us.

God is omnipotent, omniscient and omnipresent.
Never ever think you're alone.
Tip: Just focus quietly, call on His presence and welcome it as your very own Holy Spirit.

My thoughts:

_____

_____

_____

_____

DECEMBER
DAY 26

God is looking for us as Christians to show Him and others some love. In John 15:9-14, Jesus was teaching His disciples about keeping the commandments and abiding in His love. God created each one of us with a specific purpose in mind. When we walk in His purpose, we bring Him glory and joy. When we abide in Him, we bring Him praise. Let's first establish the fact that God is all love. "He who does not love does not know God, For God is Love. In this the love of God was manifested toward us, that God has sent His only begotten Son into the world that we might live through Him." [1 John 4:8]

God's Word is all about love. We need to show more love to God and our brethren.
Pure, unconditional love is given without the human expectation of any return whatsoever.
You've shown pure love many times; list the times you were happiest in showing true love.

My thoughts:

_____

_____

_____

_____

DECEMBER
DAY 27

As believers, we're immersed in the love of God because He lives in us. When we obey the commandments of the Lord, we show Him that we love and glorify Him, too. "By this My Father is glorified that you bear much fruit: so you will be my disciples." [John 15:8] The fruit we should divinely bear forth as we live out our life in Him are: listening skills, encouragement, help, and giving our service, substance and self. This pattern had already been established between God and His Son; so should it be with us, "that we love one another." Paul advised, "Love suffers long and is kind, love does not envy, love does not parade itself, is not puffed up, does not behave rudely, does not seek its own, is not provoked, thinks no evil, does not rejoice in iniquity, but rejoices in the Truth." [1 Corinthians 13] Everyone should find ourselves loving our fellow brothers and sisters in these heartfelt ways, to selflessly spread God's love throughout the world.

Sincere love of one another is a true manifestation of God's love for us.
Honor your brothers and sisters as you honor God—in selflessly giving service, substance and self whenever appropriate.
Our sweet and heartfelt efforts mean the world for everyone we interact with. Their souls will be touched and appreciate your efforts.

My thoughts:

_____

_____

_____

_____

DECEMBER
DAY 28

As we prepare for the New Year, let's honor the Lord's exhortation: "Seek Me and you will find Me." We must seek the Presence of God in all things, and in all the things we do. Jesus' presence was with the disciples on the evening after performing the miracle of feeding over 5,000 men, women and children with two fishes and five loaves of bread. Jesus asked the disciples to go over to the other side. When the disciples were preparing to cross over to the other side, a storm arose. Peter saw Jesus out on the water, and asked, "Jesus, is that you?" [Matthew 14:28-30] This year, the enemy will wage war against the people of God in even bigger ways. We must be prepared for daily battles and fight back with determination to experience the supernatural move of God. Jesus spoke just one word that gave Peter the confidence to move beyond himself into the supernatural realm of God. He commanded Peter, "Come." This coming year, you'll walk in other realms of God, too. Step up to follow the steps God has for you!

Invoke God's Word for you as you prepare for the coming year.
Pray and meditate soulfully to better feel His Presence and hear
Him divinely and properly.
Record these flashes of intuition for your New Year's resolutions.

My thoughts:

_____

_____

_____

_____

DECEMBER
DAY 29

Thomas Edison wrote, "Many of life's failures are people who did not realize how close they were to success when they gave up." Given the few setbacks over the year, count it all as joy—that you've learned a few things along the way. God can transform every setback into a set up for something great. Be reassured the devil can't stop God's plan, no matter how threatening his attacks may seem. "No weapon formed against you shall prosper." [Isaiah 54:17] Satan is aware your breakthrough is just a few meters from where you currently are. Victory is closer than you think, so don't give up. 99 percent of the race has been run. You're in the last leg of the race—which is the most unpredictable, yet most exciting, time of the race. Don't look behind you, or compare yourself to one who may have started after you. It's easy to see the leader change in the last leg. You may have paced yourself just right and run a steady race all year. Now is not the time to stop. It's time to pour it on! God could be using the very thing that seemed like a disadvantage to release new destiny into your life. So, pick up the pace and increase your speed. Just remember, when you see the finish line, give an extra stretch!

Never give up on running your best with life's great adventures. Don't sell yourself short by giving up—especially when divine victory is so very, very close!

My thoughts:

_____

_____

_____

_____

DECEMBER
DAY 30

Always seek God first. The Lord said: "He would add all things unto you." [Matthew 6:33] Seek the Lord and His strength; seek His presence continually." [1 Chronicles 16:11] May you seek and find; may you knock and many doors be opened to you; may you ask, so He responds exceedingly and abundantly—over and above all that you could ever think of, to ask!

God knows what's best for us. Ask, seek and pray for His
guidance this coming New Year.
He knows what each of us should aspire to, to manifest Him in
the Highest.
Offer gratitude to be always in His Gracious Presence.

My thoughts:
_____
_____
_____
_____

DECEMBER
DAY 31

"Praise be to the Lord, the God of Israel, from everlasting to everlasting. Amen and Amen." [Psalm 41:13] Our God is worthy to be constantly praised because He is so gracious to mankind, without exception (even though we make mistakes and stand wrong sometimes). Thank you God, for Your bountiful blessings of healing, love, good health, happiness and abundant prosperity. You alone are worthy of All the Glory, in the Highest! Amen.

God made everyone in His image—to be obedient unto Him—so we reap the blessings and rewards He has planned for us.
Rejoice at all the experiences He has experienced in and through you, good and not so good.
Give thanks to God, and be generous in showing your heartfelt appreciation to everyone.

My thoughts:

_____
_____
_____
_____

ABOUT THE AUTHOR

Michael A. Patton is the Senior Pastor, Apostle and Founder of Kingdom Life Christian Cathedral, located in South Bend Indiana. Born to the late Bobby J. Patton and Janice Hall in South Fulton, Tennessee, he grew up in the Midwest spending time in Rockford, Illinois and South Bend, Indiana. He served in the U S Air Force for six years. While stationed in the Pacific, he played semi-professional basketball. As a past interim President/CEO for the Urban League affiliate in St. Joseph County, he has worked to empower people to improve their standard of living and secure economic stability. Apostle Mike earned a bachelor's degree from Bethel College, Mishawaka, Indiana.

After receiving Christ in 1987, he began to realize the call that had been placed on his life to preach the Word of God. After some years of fervent prayer and time spent with God, he started to walk out the call that was on his life with Holy Ghost boldness and in the power of God. He teaches others to do the same.

Kingdom Life Christian Cathedral is where Apostle Michael began to walk in the mandate God had for his life teaching people with simplicity and power. His assignment is to minister to the whole person: spirit, soul and body, with emphasis on faith, the family, finances and fellowship. Apostle Michael is a powerful teacher and operates under a strong prophetic apostolic anointing. He has preached internationally in Malawi, Africa and looks forward to returning there to expand his ministry. He has a passion for spreading the good news and loves all of God's people.

He is married to Tina Patton. They have four children, Brittany, Devin, Tobias and Jada. Visit www.kingdomlifeccc.org.